CW00662411

CUBA

SPIRALGUIDE

AA Publishing

Contents

Original text by Andrew Forbes
Revised and updated by Jane Egginton

Project Editor Linda Miles
Project Designer Alison Fenton
Series Editor Karen Rigden

Published by AA Publishing, a trading name of AA Media Limited,
whose registered office is Fanum House, Basing View, Basingstoke,
Hampshire, RG21 4EA. Registered number 06112600.

ISBN: 978-0-7495-7168-9

We have tried to ensure accuracy in this guide, but things do
change, so please let us know if you have any comments at
travelguides@theAA.com.

A CIP catalogue record for this book is available from the
British Library.

Cover design and binding style by permission of AA Publishing
Colour separation by AA Digital Department
Printed and bound in China by Leo Paper Products

Find out more about AA Publishing and the wide range of travel
publications and services the AA provides by visiting our website
at theAA.com/shop

A04601
Maps in this title produced from mapping © Freytag-Berndt
u.Artaria KG, 1231 Vienna-Austria.

The Magazine

A great holiday is more than just lying on a beach or shopping till you drop — to really get the most from your trip you need to know what makes the place tick. The Magazine provides an entertaining overview to some of the social, cultural and natural elements that make up the unique character of this engaging country.

Where
RHYTHM RULES

Cuba is universally renowned for its pervasive, complex musical rhythms. It doesn't seem to matter whether it's rain or shine – a street party, a fiesta, a religious ceremony, a bar, nightclub or even a funeral – the music never stops.

Musical Roots

At the very heart of Cuban musical tradition lie the complex percussive rhythms of West and Central Africa. The most important of these is probably that of the Yoruba people (➤ 16), one of the three great tribes of modern Nigeria. To this has been added the sophisticated music of Spain, based on forms that are as much Berber and Arab as they are Castilian and Basque. Add a touch of French musical tradition – especially from around Cienfuegos (➤ 102–105), where many refugees from the

1791 Slave Rebellion in Haiti settled – plus a natural flood of joy, lively celebration of femininity and virtual surfeit of machismo, and you have the roots, at least, of Cuba's unique, vibrant and inescapable music.

The Sounds of Son

Most contemporary music in Cuba is based on son, a form of Latino "country music" believed to have originated in the east of the country in the 19th century. Over the intervening years it has grown more and more sophisticated, with instruments such as horns, flutes and fiddles added to the original combination of guitar, bongo, double bass and – central to just about all Cuban music and creating a rhythm that's impossible to ignore – the *claves*, two ridged sticks rubbed or beaten together to mark the beat.

External Influences

By the 1940s, son had given rise to more complex, larger sounds, such as rumba, mambo and chá-chá-chá. In the mid-20th century (and not entirely unrelated to the growing emigrant community in the US following Castro's 1959 revolution), salsa emerged as a universally popular form of expression across North America and beyond. In the 1980s, an unexpected but positive input to Cuban music was made when it was exposed to Ethiopian and Angolan musical forms during Castro's lengthy military interventions on behalf of the socialist regimes in those countries.

Dancers at Cabaret Tropicana in Havana, one of Cuba's most exciting music venues

On the way to a gig in Trinidad de Cuba

Hip Hop, Rap and Reggaeton

Hip hop and rap made its way into Cuba from Miami in the early 1990s via crackly radio transmissions and is now one of the most popular forms of music on the island. The Cuban Rap Agency was set up by the state to nurture its homegrown talent. Reggaeton, a heady combination of reggae, Latin and electronic music, exploded onto the island's musical scene in 2000. The sexually charged lyrics that glorify materialism, yet address the country's pressing social issues, have polarized the Cuban community. Today, reggaeton is the most popular form of music on the island.

All Singing, All Dancing

Cuban music is generally joyful, and Cubans really do dance in the streets – not just young people moving apparently effortlessly (and often sensually) at street-side parties, but older people waltzing happily in the many parks that distinguish most Cuban cities. Cubans – long driven to exasperation by the capricious economic policies of their government – like to say that music, dancing and making love are the main activities that make life tolerable.

MUSICAL HOUSES

One way to witness this extraordinary musical experience (other than just walking the streets) is to visit a Casa de la Trova (House of Troubadours) in Havana, Santiago de Cuba (► 150), or Trinidad (► 124). Casas de la Música (Houses of Music) are also found in most – if not all – Cuban cities, including Havana (► 71) and Trinidad (► 124). Here musicians sing and play everything from son to salsa to traditional *trova* (ballads) all day and much of the night. Cubans love – adore – their music, and will rarely miss an opportunity to go to endless lengths to explain and encourage the complex yet driving rhythms to enthusiastic outsiders.

HECHO en CUBA

If Cuba is famous for two products other than the ubiquitous sugar that blankets most of the island, they are rum and cigars. *"Hecho en Cuba"* (Made in Cuba) is proudly stamped on every bottle, box and label.

A Potent Brew

Rum is a direct product (though certainly not the only one) of the island's great swathes of sugar fields and tall, smoke-belching sugar mills. To produce rum – or *ron* as it is known in Cuba – local distilleries take the highest quality molasses or *miel de cana* (cane honey) and dilute it with water, adding yeast and allowing the mix to ferment for around 30 hours.

Refining the Flavour

The fermented brew is then heated before being allowed to condense in a copper vat. Generally the resultant liquor is tested and either strengthened or weakened until it is around 75 per cent proof. The young rum is then stored in oak barrels and allowed to mature for three, five or even seven years. Various ingredients, from caramel to baby guavas, may be added to the young rum to produce different flavours.

Classic Cocktails

The result is quite a drink, and distinctively Cuban – at least when served in such famous cocktails as the daiquirí (a blend of rum, lemon juice, sugar, maraschino and crushed iced, shaken rather than stirred), the Cuba Libre (rum, cola and crushed ice, stirred rather than shaken) or mojito (a refreshing blend of mint, lime, sugar, soda and rum).

A refreshing mojito (top) and a fine cigar (bottom), a classic Cuban combination

A Revolutionary Move

The famous Barcardi rum had been distilled in Santiago de Cuba since 1878, but the Barcardi family were no socialists. After Castro's seizure of power in 1959, the company departed for nearby Puerto Rico. The old factory in Santiago produces the well-known Caney brand and in 2011 launched Caney 12 Años, a new premium rum which is aged for 12 years.

A Rum Tour

Visitors should not miss the highly elaborate art nouveau Edificio Bacardí building, the company's former headquarters, just east of Havana's Parque Central – and only a short walk from Ernest Hemingway's old watering holes of El Floridita and La Bodeguita del Medio (➤ 67), both admittedly touristy but enjoyable stop-offs for a rum cocktail or two. Nearby, the excellent Museo del Ron (Rum Museum) (➤ 55, 56) provides a splendid overview of rum production. At the Havana Club bar that adjoins the museum, get one of the skilled cocktail bar men, known as *cantineros,* to mix something up for you, or go for a *Cata Vertical* – a sampling of rums from youngest to oldest.

Cigar Country

Cuban cigars are generally agreed to be the best in the world. Whether rolled by machine or by hand, all of the cigars are stamped *"Hecho en Cuba"* (Made in Cuba). The finest cigar tobacco on the island is said to come from Pinar del Río (➤ 78–80) in the west of the island, and especially from Vuelta Abajo (➤ 87). The secondary region, also known as Vuelta Abajo, is in the gently undulating lands of Villa Clara province, northeast of Santa Clara.

A tobacco farmer inspects his crop in the Valle de Viñales

Visiting the Producers

Cuban *torcedoras* (cigar rollers) – most of them women – are generally agreed to be the best in the world and their work is regarded as an art form. The best place to observe the tobacco harvest and cigar manufacturing process is in the Valle de Viñales (► 154) and nearby Vuelta Abajo (► 87). Alternatively, visitors can also witness the production process and make purchases from the restored and extremely elegant Partagás Factory, west of Central Havana's Parque Central (► 60–61).

Famous Names

For decades names such as Cohiba, Montecristo and Romeo y Julieta have been celebrated worldwide, not least for their popularity with the rich, famous and powerful. Examples that spring readily to mind are Winston Churchill, Groucho Marx and John F. Kennedy – the latter ordered 1,200 of the very best Cuban cigars from an aide in Washington the day before he signed the anti-Cuban embargo bill. Yet another famous cigar smoker was Fidel Castro himself. Fidel gave up smoking in 1985, commenting "they're good for the country, but not for my health".

Going Up In Smoke?

The global recession and anti-smoking laws have hit the cigar industry hard. In 2009, the number of cigars exported plummeted to 73 million from 217 million in 2006. Yet, cigars remain big business for Cuba (even without the US market) and the industry continues to push for new markets. In 2010, the Julieta cigar, the milder, smaller sister of the well-known Romeo y Julieta, was launched in a bold move to attract more women cigar smokers.

Cigars in production at the Partagás Factory in Havana

Origins of a Nation

Much of Cuba's history lies buried forever in its deep past. A great deal of the country's original indigenous Amerindian culture was destroyed by the ferocious, gold-seeking, god-preaching Conquistadors.

Early Settlers

Archaeologists believe the first human beings may have reached Cuba as long ago as 3500BC. These earliest settlers were Amerindian people known as the Guanahatabey, who settled mainly in the west of the island, and the Siboney, who occupied the east. As far as we can tell, they lived mainly by fishing and hunting. It was not until around AD1000 that they were joined by the more numerous Taíno people, refugee agriculturalists from the nearby Caribbean island of Hispaniola – the gentle Taíno usually lost out in territorial fights to the Caribs, the famously ferocious Indians, after whom the Caribbean was named. The Taíno were driven farther and farther west, but they were still inhabiting the island of Cuba in great numbers when the Europeans arrived in the 16th century.

Taino villagers fish for turtles as Columbus's ships approach the island

Columbus and Cortez

On 28 October 1492, the navigator Christopher Columbus first made landfall at Gibara (➤ 141), on the northeast coast of Cuba. He was immediately struck by the innocence of the Taíno Indians whom he said would grasp a sword by its blade. Columbus declared the island "the most beautiful land human eyes have ever seen" and decided it was part of Asia. Following a circumnavigation of the island in 1508, this was proved to be a serious misconception; it was left to the explorer Hernán Cortés, 30 years later, to cross the Isthmus of Panama and stare "with a wild surmise" on sighting the Pacific Ocean.

Spanish Colonialism

The Spaniards returned to Cuba in 1512, when an expedition led by Diego de Velázquez – Cuba's first governor – landed at Baracoa, founded the first settlement, and began the island's long colonial servitude. The bust of one of the first independence martyrs, the Indian chief Hatuey, who was burned alive by the Spanish invaders, still stands outside the church at Baracoa.

> "the most beautiful land human eyes have ever seen"

Cuba was to prove a disappointment to the early gold-hungry Conquistadors. There wasn't much gold to be found, local Amerindians died in droves from disease and overwork, and religious conversions failed – Hatuey declined to be baptized before his execution on the (reasonable) grounds that he didn't want to see such cruel Spaniards again, even in heaven.

Growth of Industry

Cuba did serve the Conquistadors in another way – as a source of fresh meat and food, as well as a departure point for the ongoing enterprise of conquering Mexico and Perú. Following the decimation of the native Indians, the Spanish turned increasingly to African slaves as a source of labour. The first were brought over as early as the mid-16th century. Over the next two centuries, Cuba developed as a vital source of cattle, tobacco and sugar cane. Havana evolved as a wealthy port, thanks not least to the Spanish treasure fleets that gathered for the dangerous journey to Europe.

European Influence

Not that Spain's supremacy in the Caribbean would remain unchallenged for long. Other European nations – France, the Netherlands, and most notably Britain – harassed Spanish galleons and ransacked Cuban cities, which were regularly attacked by legally sanctioned pirates and buccaneers. In 1762, the British seized Havana and held sway over Cuba for a year (during which they opened the island to international trade) before swapping the island for Florida.

American Interest

Between 1810 and 1825, under the guidance of the great statesman and liberator Simón Bolívar, mainland South America won independence from Spain, leaving only "loyal Cuba" as Spain's major possession in the region. Part of the reason for this loyalty was fear of the African slaves, who now dominated much of the country. In 1791, a slave revolt in neighbouring Haiti resulted in the overthrow of French power and the flight of thousands of white settlers, terrifying many Cuban Whites, whose slogan became "better a Spanish Cuba than a Black Cuba". Meanwhile, the fast-maturing US eagle was flexing its imperial wings. In 1848, Washington offered Madrid US$100 million to buy Cuba, raising the offer in 1854 to US$130 million. The Spanish foreign minister refused, declaring he would "rather see Cuba sink beneath the waves". However, the writing was on the wall, and the days of Spanish dominion were numbered.

A statue of Carlos Manuel de Céspedes who declared independence from Spain

Independence from Spain

In 1868, Spain's high-handed attitude and colonial arrogance towards native-born creoles sparked the long-delayed revolt. It started in the traditionally rebellious east of the island, as far from Spanish-influenced Havana as possible. Among the numerous Cuban independence fighters who emerged from the resulting Wars of Independence, two stand head and shoulders above the rest.

Fidel Castro fought against Batista

The first was Carlos Manuel de Céspedes (1819–78), viewed by Cubans as the first national hero of their independence. On 10 October 1868, he rang the great bell on his sugar estate at La Demajagua, near Manzanillo, announcing the freedom of his slaves, as well as Cuba's declaration of independence from Spain. The event sparked the brutal Ten Year War, from which Spain emerged victorious.

The second and greatest of all Cuban national heroes was the independence leader José Martí (1853–95). He was sentenced to hard labour, and later exiled for his nationalist activities. In 1881, he arrived in New York, where he worked tirelessly for the nationalist cause, and emerged as its undisputed leader. He returned to Cuba in 1895 to lead the War of Independence, but was killed without firing a single shot during his first skirmish with the Spanish occupiers. Nevertheless, today there is a bust of Martí, "the sincere man from the land of the palm tree", in towns and villages throughout Cuba.

The Eagle has Landed

Soon after, the American domination that Martí had foreseen came to pass. In 1898, following the still unexplained sinking of the battleship USS *Maine* off Havana Harbour, the US declared war on Spain and quickly seized control not just of Cuba but of Puerto Rico, Guam and the Philippines. Cuban aspirations for self-determination were thwarted. Although it "granted" Cuba independence, during the next five decades the US controlled a series of corrupt dictators. US big business ran the Cuban economy, while American gangsters and high-rollers used Havana as their personal, exotic playground.

In 1952, power was seized by a corrupt, pro-US army sergeant called Fulgencio Batista, who proclaimed himself dictator and ran Cuba for his own profit and that of his US cronies. In this way, the stage for the Cuban Revolution was already set (➤ 20–22).

SANTERÍA

Cuba is considered a Catholic country. The influence of Catholic Spain set the official backdrop for Cuba's social and religious framework. Yet, under the surface, Cuban blood courses with the influence of Santería.

Way of the Saints

Santería, or the "way of the saints", has transformed Cuban Catholicism to an extent that it is now probably the main religion among Cubans. Its influence is pervasive at all levels of society, and this influence has grown rather than diminished, despite government efforts to usurp it.

African Roots

Santería originated among the Yoruba people of Nigeria – the main source of slave labour imported during the colonial years to raise sugar cane and perform other back-breaking tasks in the Cuban countryside.

Like so many facets of Cuban society, Santería is the product of two inextricably opposed and yet remarkably similar traditions. The Spanish masters forbade slaves to practise their "heathen" religion, known as Regla de Ocha, a belief system which acknowledges numerous orisha, or gods, in a way not entirely dissimilar to the cannon of saints recognized by the Catholic Church.

A New Faith

In Santería, Olofi is the supreme god, but he is remote and cannot be approached directly. Rather, supplicants must approach him through lesser divinities – the orisha, who represent both the forces of nature and the human condition. Santería recognizes hundreds of orishas, but some are more important than others.

Standing on Ceremony

Traditionally, Santería devotees wear white clothing and elaborate necklaces. Music, dance, spirit possession and animal sacrifice are all ways of communicating with orishas during initiations and feasts. These very private ceremonies held for birth, marriages and deaths, or for healing, take place in halls or private homes.

Santería is practised widely across Cuba, but it remains a very private form of worship

For the visitor, it's easy to see the outward trappings of this Afro-Cuban religion. Santería women dance in the Plaza des Armas in La Habana Vieja, while cigar-smoking priestesses pose for photographs. Yet the real essence of Santería remains mysterious – the casual visitor will find it difficult to witness authentic ceremonies, and it may take many months of patient enquiries to meet serious initiates. The Havana suburbs of Regla and Guanabacoa are the most important centres of Santería practice.

Santería has a significant following in the US, among not only the black and Hispanic population but also whites and Asians. Some Spanish Catholics adopt elements of Santería belief, including personal shrines in their houses, where simple offerings of rum are made as suppliants.

Religious Revolution

The Revolution and the religion of Santería have always been closely entwined; when the revolutionaries emerged from the mountains of the Sierra Maestra, many of them were wearing the distinctive, brightly coloured Santería beads. Many followers even credit Castro with the ability to protect them, his people. Famously, when a white dove settled on the leader's shoulder at a political rally soon after he took power, many took it as a sign that he had been blessed by the gods; some even credit him with the ability to avert major hurricanes.

Catholic Cuba

Cuba remains an essentially Catholic country and, in 1998, Pope John Paul II made an historic visit to the island. The country's first orthodox church opened in 2008, with Raúl Castro present at the ceremony. Christmas has been celebrated since 1998 (it was banned in 1969 when the country was declared atheist) but the biggest festival in Cuba remains New Year's Eve, which is a time of ritual cleansing of homes and when high priests of Santería make their predictions for the following year.

THE MAFIA
CONNECTION

Between the US "liberation" of Cuba from Spanish rule in 1898 and the overthrow of Batista in 1959, Cuba became a hub for US military, business and Mafia connections.

Yankee Stranglehold

Territorial control by the US at Guantánamo Bay dates from the early years of the 20th century, as does American corporate domination of Cuban sugar and tobacco. Despite the granting of independence in 1902, Cuba remained a US colony in all but name for the next six decades. Meanwhile, the US Mafia took over Havana and made it their playground.

Havana's Heyday

The beginnings of Havana's reputation as a sin city came during the time of the US Prohibition in the 1920s. Cuba emerged as a convenient offshore hub not just of alcohol consumption, but also of prostitution and gambling. The mob moved in big time, buying up hotels, establishing casinos and building flashy houses in Havana.

Setting Up Shop

After 1938, when Fulgencio Batista first seized power, mob power grew. Batista invited Meyer Lansky, the "Jewish Godfather", to take over the

running of the casino and racetrack businesses. Gambling flourished. The mob made a fortune, and massive kickbacks were paid to Batista.

In December 1946, the biggest Mafia convention since the Depression was held in Havana. Nearly every Mafia family boss from the US attended the event. Meanwhile, the Cuban peasants sweated and slaved for peanuts. However, many Cubans, including a young law student called Fidel Castro, knew what was going on and bitterly resented the exploitation of their country by mobsters.

Fidel Plots his Revenge

In 1953, Castro and a band of compatriots launched a doomed attack on the Moncada Barracks in Santiago de Cuba (➤ 136). A year later, when the young firebrand Castro was serving time in prison, Batista appointed Lansky his "personal adviser on gambling reform".

Under Batista, efforts were made to promote tax-free tourism. Almost every hotel had a casino, and so profitable did the business become that even educated Cubans, such as doctors and teachers, gave up their jobs to become croupiers.

Mobsters' Retreat

During these years, Lansky deposited more than US$3 million in Batista's personal bank accounts in Switzerland. All this ended on New Year's Eve 1958. As Castro's forces scented victory, Batista fled with a suitcase full of gold, and lived in Portugal until his death in 1973. One of Castro's first acts was to warn the mobsters, particularly Lansky: "not only will we prosecute gangsters," he thundered, "we will certainly shoot them." Said Lansky, who had just opened the Hotel Riviera and casino: "I crapped out!" Lansky fled to the Bahamas, where he is said to have offered a bounty on Castro's head. Within months, Cuba's casinos were closed.

Gamblers at a gaming table in a Havana casino in 1932

Los BARBUDOS

From 1959 to 2011, strongman Fidel Castro dominated
Cuban politics, a position made more secure by the
personality cult surrounding the charismatic but long dead
Ernesto "Che" Guevara. Indeed, Fidel was the longest-
ruling leader in the Western world, and the irony is that few
people believed he would be there that long were it not for
continuing and unyielding US opposition to his rule.

Unshaven warriors Fidel Castro (opposite) and Che Guevara, the faces of revolution

The illegitimate third of seven children of an affluent sugar farmer, Fidel Castro Ruz was born in 1927 in Finca Las Manacas in Eastern Cuba, where his mother was the household maid. He attended Catholic and Jesuit schools before studying law at Havana University where, in the company of other like-minded young revolutionaries, he concluded the dictator Fulgencio Batista (➤ 15, 19) must be overthrown by force.

A Force to be Reckoned With

Castro's first attempt was staged on 26 July 1953, at the Moncada Barracks (➤ 136) in Santiago de Cuba. It failed militarily owing to the rebels being hugely outnumbered. "Convict me," he told his judges. "What does it matter? History will absolve me." After a period of imprisonment on the Isla de la Juventud, he went into exile, where he met the young Argentinean doctor Ernesto "Che" Guevara and set up an army in training. In 1956, they sailed for Cuba on the motor launch *Granma* (➤ 53), arriving at Playa del Colorado in the southwest of the island. This time, after a prolonged guerrilla struggle in both mountains and cities, they were victorious and the Batista regime was replaced by Castro and his politically committed and youthful revolutionaries.

The Bearded Ones

In the idealistic spirit of the times, Los Barbudos (The Bearded Ones), as these unshaven warriors were called, soon became icons for a generation. Guevara was the son of middle-class Argentinean parents. He gave up a career in medicine to spread revolution and anti-imperialism across the world. His handsome features, austerity and extreme discipline inspired tremendous loyalty and love for him among his followers, and not a little admiration from women. In fact, Guevara was – no doubt he had to be

– quite ruthless. In reality, he ordered many executions, even carrying out some personally. Che was captured and executed by Bolivian soldiers in 1967, while leading a guerilla movement in Bolivia. His handsome features became the perfect – and continuing – icon for the Cuban Revolution. As a consequence, a Guevara cult has developed. Castro, who continues to represent Che as a model of selfless sacrifice, has carefully nurtured this. The saintly image of Che is seen everywhere, generally accompanied by his most famous maxim – "Always Onwards to Victory!" Meanwhile, billboards and

Che Guevara making a radio speech at rebel headquarters in the 1950s

wall murals are adorned with "Socialism or death!" slogans accompanying images of Castro, who ran Cuba with endless calls for greater sacrifice, although any image of him is noticeably absent.

Local Feeling

Cubans are bitterly divided in their opinions of the two men. Just about everybody, apart from party members and very close associates, can see that the economic process championed by the Revolution has completely failed. Cuba is in a far worse state of poverty than it should be, and this is in major part due to failed socialist policies. However, there's the US economic blockade to take into consideration, too – it seems unfairly disproportionate to Castro's "excesses", and many Cubans consider it both petty and vindictive. Besides, no real Cuban patriot – even if an exile living on Florida's Palm Beach – wants to see their lovely island become just another colonial adjunct of the US.

The 21st Century

There is real pride in some of the achievements of the Cuban Revolution (notably in education, health and a progressive value system that nurtures positive virtues), as well as genuine despair at its economic and social failures. Most Cubans were probably happy to see Castro go when he formally resigned in 2011 – but are relieved that the process arrived naturally and without the US seizing back control of the island.

El Comandante, or *El Jefe Máximo* (The Maximum Chief) – as Castro was styled – handed over power in 2008, to his younger brother Raúl, when he became too ill to govern. Head of the Cuban armed forces and a gifted manager, Raúl is now officially Cuba's ruler and has delivered on his promise to provide a less ideological, more pragmatic, style of leadership.

Cuba
TODAY

Life for Cubans is changing at a rate of knots. As President Raúl Castro says, "we are on the edge of a precipice" – the country is opening up, and now is a great time to visit.

La Lucha ("The Struggle")

More than 50 years after Fidel took power, ordinary Cubans have learned to work within the constraints of the Revolution. With strict rationing of food and basic necessities, the people have learned to waste nothing. Ancient, dying refrigerators are coaxed back to life, clothes are endlessly recycled, and the oldest Nintendo consoles are treasured possessions, passed down across generations of children. To make ends meet, every family seeks a second revenue stream, and preferably one that pays in hard currency.

On package tours, visitors are coached to be wary of *jineteros* – "jockeys", or locals who make a living on the back of tourists. This covers a whole range of conduct from street cons to prostitution. However, while these activities do take place, they are not common and crimes against tourists attract harsh penalties. So, visitors should be open to contact with ordinary Cubans (panel ► 24).

Top: President Raúl Castro greets elderly revolutionaries at the 26 July celebrations
Middle: A classic American Dodge taxi
Bottom: Catching up on the news in Santa Clara

MEET THE CUBANS

Package holidays are the norm for most people visiting Cuba. Should you wish to experience something more "real" then the following are great, mutually enriching ways to achieve this.

■ One popular source of tourist dollars is the *casa particular*, where a local family rents out a spare room in their house. This is a wonderful, enlightening experience for the visitor – a chance to live as the locals do, enjoy their warm hospitality, and chat with them openly.

■ In bars and restaurants, appearances can be deceptive, and it's not uncommon for your waiter to be working their second job and for them to be highly over-qualified – you might even discover they're a university professor. While your tips help feed their family, most are also keen to learn about the outside world, and to glimpse the freedoms we take for granted.

■ There are only limited jobs in the official tourist industry, so many people look to "invent". The often feared *jinetero* (▶ 23) may be just a young man offering to drive you round Havana in his uncle's vintage car – trust your instincts and common sense.

■ Another source of income and foreign contact are *paladares*. These are little restaurants in private family homes, typically open for a few hours in the evening. They are permitted by the state, which takes a hefty chunk of the revenue as tax. For the visitor, a night out in a *paladar*, with fresh home-cooked food in an intimate atmosphere, is a welcome change from the state-run hotel restaurants.

Walls have Ears

Within the cosy confines of your hotel, it's easy to escape the effects of the pervasive nature of the government, but a little knowledge of the situation goes a long way to helping you to understand how it affects your hosts. Each neighbourhood is controlled by its local CDR (Committee of the Defence of the Revolution). These august bodies monitor local people's zeal (or lack of it) for the Revolution. Critical comments are frowned upon and can damage employment, education and housing opportunities for the entire family. For this reason, visitors should not try to engage locals in open discussion about politics in public. Be sensitive and take time to get to know the Cuban people. Learn to read between the lines, and reserve any criticisms for quieter, more private moments.

The Future

In 2008, Castro stepped down as president owing to ill health and Raúl – his calmer although less charismatic younger brother – took over. Raúl aims to make his mark by forging a new direction for the country. A recent change has seen increased support for farmers in the small private agricultural sector. Controls on businesses are being relaxed and self-employment is being encouraged. To ease Havana's commuter

A vintage car on the motorway

chaos, Raúl imported a fleet of buses from China, and Cubans have even been allowed to own mobile phones and computers (although most still can't afford to run them).

Raúl has made no secret of the fact that Cuba cannot sustain the current level of subsidies. He scrapped the monthly handout of four packs of cigarettes given to all Cubans over the age of 54 and there are plans to lay off one million workers – a fifth of the working population – by 2016. The hope is that they will find employment in the burgeoning private sector.

All of these developments reflect the leadership's gradual grudging acceptance that change is needed. Consumerism and economic freedoms are certainly coming, and it is hoped that democracy and press freedom may follow.

ON THE ROAD

The country's main *autopista* (motorway) runs from Pinar del Río, via Havana to Santiago in the west. Cubans are very proud of it, but it is potholed and unlit, sometimes descending into a dirt-track, and used by bicycles and horses as much as cars and trucks. In the countryside, buses are few and far between, with most people walking or hitchhiking to work. If you decide to hire a car and drive outside Havana, expect to come across hitchhikers, almost all of whom are perfectly respectable people just trying to get from A to B. Unfortunately, the government doesn't like locals hitching rides from tourists, so police may stop the car to check their ID, though visitors will never be harassed.

Sporting CUBANS

For a country with a population of only around 11 million people, Cuba certainly punches above its weight, at least as far as sports are concerned.

Cuba has produced many world-class athletes and sporting heroes. Much of this great achievement has occurred since Fidel Castro banned professional sport in 1962. The Olympics, with its amateur charter, was the perfect stage for Cuban sporting prowess. Many Cuban Olympians had made their mark long before Castro – for example, the 1904 Cuban fencing team won every medal available apart from the sabre event – but the Revolution signalled the rise of Cuban sporting might.

Boxing Clever

Boxers began to dominate the Olympics at all weights. The film *Sons of Cuba* (2009) examined the boxing phenomenon in the country, following nine-year-olds on a boxing boot camp and offering an insight into the country's success in the sport. Since 1972, Cuba has taken home 32 of the 104 boxing gold medals available, despite boycotting the games in 1984 and 1988. Probably the two best-known boxers to the outside world were both heavyweights. Teófilo Stevenson, a giant of a man, was champion in 1972, 1976 and 1980, and would undoubtedly have won again in 1984 had Cuba attended the Los Angeles games.

Going for Gold

Once the Cubans rejoined the Olympics in 1992, another heavyweight waded in. Félix Savón went on to become champion in 1992, 1996 and 2000. Famous US boxing promoter Don King tried to coax him into becoming a professional, offering him a staggering US$10 million: Savon's reply, "What do I need $10 million for when I have 11 million Cubans behind me?" Even at the 2004 Athens Olympics, Cuban boxers won five gold medals, but since then the country's standing has been weakened by a series of defections that has seen young athletes fleeing the country. In 2006, three of the country's reigning Olympic boxing champions sold their

Left to right: Dayron Robles at the Beijing Olympics; *Sons of Cuba*; baseball is king

medals to buy food for their family and then escaped from a training camp in Venezuela. In 2008 at Beijing, for the first time, Cuba did not qualify a boxer in all 11 Olympic weight classes. As Cuba boxing trainer, Roberto Quesada, who now lives in Miami, put it: "Gold medals are wonderful, but athletes can't eat their gold medals."

Runaway Success

Athletics have also produced some highs, most famously at the 1976 Montréal Olympics, where an unknown Cuban, Alberto Juantorena, ran away with gold medals in the 400m and 800m, an unprecedented feat. On his return to Havana, Juantorena spent the next 15 days cutting sugar cane; even sporting heroes are part of the revolutionary struggle. Women have had similar successes. María Colón won the javelin gold medal at the 1980 Moscow Olympics, the first non-European to win for almost 50 years.

First Base

Cuban teams outshine even the US at baseball. Baseball aficionados will argue that the Cuban teams at the Olympic Games in Barcelona in 1992 and again in Atlanta in 1996 were perhaps the greatest baseball teams of all time, although 1997 saw the end of a 10-year winning streak. Since then, however, the country has been dogged by defections.

The Politics of Play

Sport in Cuba has always been linked with the politics of the country, where international success is constantly used to promote socialist ideals. It is also integral to health and education. Cuban coaches are employed around the world, but within the country, training and investment remains a priority. In recent years, Fidel has substituted his traditional military combats for a Nike tracksuit bearing the slogan: "Just Do It".

IN THE WILD

Cuba boasts unique diversity in its landscapes and wildlife – from the farms and villages of the Viñales National Park (▶ 154) and the scenic mountains of the Gran Parque Nacional Sierra Maestra (▶ 166–167) to the spectacular coral-rich dive sites dotted all around its coast.

Eco-tourism

The country's burgeoning, although still relatively undeveloped, eco-tourism scene offers horse-riding and trekking trips, and a variety of tours on water and on land. Rare Cuban crocodiles, Caribbean manatees and native nesting turtles can all be seen in their natural habitat. Among Cuba's national parks, reserves and protected areas, the largest is the Ciénaga de Zapata Biosphere Reserve (▶ 89) at 15,000ha (1.5 million acres), a wetland of international importance and refuge for many species of aquatic birds.

Environmental Record

Cuba in some ways is years ahead of many supposedly more "developed" countries. Organic farming and recycling (the sugar mills are run on re-used sugar cane) are nothing new to the country. However, the island's environmental record is far from clean – the endangered Hawksbill turtles were hunted until 2008, for example, and many forested areas have suffered severe degradation, and a large number of the country's rivers are contaminated by pollutants.

Left to right: Fairy basslet; Cuban tree frog; Caribbean flamingo

Bird watching

More than 350 species of bird have been recorded on the island, from the rare bee hummingbird, the smallest bird in the world found only in Cuba, to the common white egret. Visitors can see pretty, pink flamingoes at Laguna de las Salinas, Gran Parque Natural Montemar (➤ 89) and may catch sight of the red, white and blue Cuban Trogon, which has been designated the country's national bird, as it has the same colours as the country's flag. Dedicated birders can take specialist bird-watching tours.

Fishing

Cuba's finest waters for deep-sea fishing, including sailfish, swordfish, tuna, barracuda and shark, are found along the northwest coast, where the Gulf Stream flows through the Straits of Florida. These waters, much loved by angler and sportsman Ernest Hemingway (➤ 30–31), include the Golfo de Guanahacabibes and the waters off Cojímar (➤ 63).

Diving and Snorkelling

Cuba's spectacular dive sites, with excellent year-round visibility, really are world class. Visitors can explore an underwater world of pristine coral reefs, fascinating marine life and impressive wrecks from Spanish galleons to Soviet submarines. Among the best are the Bahía de Corrientes off Guanahacabibes, Cayo Largo in the Archipiélago de Canarreos (➤ 82–83) and the Bahía de Cochinos (➤ 89), west of Cienfuegos.

Unspoiled Scenery

Cuba is full of wonderful drives, walks, treks and bicycle trips, across undeveloped, sparsely settled territory where you are more likely to see an ox-drawn cart or a cattle train than a tour bus. The drive around the Sierra Maestra (➤ 166–168), taking in Pico Turquino (➤ 167, 168), the highest peak, and the Valle de Viñales (➤ 153–154), tobacco country surrounded by dramatic geological formations, must rank near the top.

FORCE OF NATURE

The whole of the Caribbean island lies within the hurricane belt, with the hurricane season running from June to October. One of the worst years for hurricanes in Cuba's history was 2008. The country was ravaged by the destructive trio of Gustav, Ike and Paloma, which caused billions of dollars worth of damage and made millions of people homeless. The loss of life was minimal, thanks mostly to Cuba's highly efficient and well-developed defence system, which includes early warnings and evacuation programmes.

HEMINGWAY
and GREENE

Cuba is closely associated with two Anglo literary giants, Ernest Hemingway and Graham Greene. Interestingly, it is the macho, hunting, shooting and fishing Hemingway who seems to capture all the plaudits, while the more intellectual, sympathetic and, frankly, engaging Greene receives relatively little attention.

Ernest "Papa" Hemingway

For more than 20 years, Hemingway made Havana and its immediate environs his home, drinking in well-known watering-holes, such as El Floridita and La Bodeguita del Medio (➤ 67). He was a passionate deep-sea fisherman, hanging out at Cojímar (➤ 63) and sailing his luxurious yacht, *El Pilar*, up and down the Florida Straits looking for marlin and (during World War II, between 1941 and 1945, German submarines.

Ernest Hemingway on a fishing trip in 1940

The Old Man and the Sea

Some of Hemingway's most famous works were penned in Cuba, most notably *The Old Man and the Sea* (1952), which won the Nobel Peace Prize two years later. Initially he made his home at Hotel Ambos Mundos (➤ 64) on Calle Obsipo in La Habana Vieja, though later he bought a ranch, Finca La Vigía (➤ 63), where he lived with this third wife Martha Gelhorn. A difficult man, much given to drinking and fighting, he was nevertheless popular with most Cubans (including, apparently, Fidel Castro), and remains one of this nation's most-loved Americans.

Talking Politics

Hemingway's attitude toward the Cuban Revolution remains unclear, with both pro- and anti-Castro factions claiming his support. In fact, he seems to have welcomed the overthrow of the dictator Batista, describing the *Fidelistas* as "honest revolutionaries" in a letter to a friend, and commenting on the flight

> "Papa is a literary and political hero who struck a chord with Cubans"

of Batista: "There goes the son of a bitch!" On the other hand, he seems to have been anxious that the US administration should not push Castro into the Soviet camp.

Hemingway left Cuba in 1960 – having been diagnosed with inoperable cancer – and committed suicide in his native Idaho a year later. He is thought to have met with Castro only once, during a deep-sea fishing contest, when he presented the young Cuban leader with the prize for catching the biggest fish.

Hemingway's Legacy

Still, Hemingway remains an ex-post-facto hero of the Cuban leadership and a powerful pull for the tourist business. There's a well-established Hemingway Trail encompassing the Hotel Ambos Mundos, the two bars – El Floridita and La Bodeguita del Medio – the Hemingway Museum at Finca La Vigía, 10km (6 miles) south of central Havana, his home, which he donated to the Cuban people, La Terraza restaurant at Cojímar (➤ 68), and the large Marina Hemingway to the west of Havana, which actually had nothing to do with the man, but was named as a tribute to him.

"Papa", as he is affectionately known, is indeed something of a literary and political hero whose machismo certainly struck a chord with many Cubans.

A hunting trophy looms over Hemingway's desk

Graham Greene (left) chats to actor Alec Guinness on the set of *Our Man in Havana*

Graham Greene

Englishman Greene was of a quite different character to Hemingway, more sophisticated and, indeed, more cynical. *Our Man in Havana* (1958), which subsequently became a film, opera and play and is Greene's percipient novel of life in Batista's Cuba, may also have cut a little close to the bone. It recounts how a British secret service agent, Jim Wormold, invents the presence of weapons of mass destruction hidden in the Cuban countryside both to please his masters and to improve his own finances.

Political Incorrectness

The novel *Our Man in Havana*, though written just a year before Batista's overthrow, may have come uncomfortably close to the mark when Soviet nuclear missiles were discovered in Cuba in 1962. Be this as it may, Fidel Castro condoned the book (though he denied it adequately represented the evils of the Batista regime) and approved its filming in Cuba. The real subject was the mocking of the British secret service, and as a comedy, Greene admitted himself that it did not fully represent the brutality of the Batista regime: "Alas, the book did me little good with the new rulers in Havana. In poking fun at the British secret service, I had minimized the terror of Batista's rule."

Speaking his Mind

For his part, Greene had a judicious respect for Castro. "In all Castro's speeches there is a sense of a man thinking aloud. He explains his course of actions, he admits mistakes... one has the sense that he respects the intelligence of his audience." Greene was less enthusiastic about Hemingway and his lifestyle, however. After visiting the latter's home at Finca La Vigía, he felt moved to comment: "taxidermy everywhere. Buffalo heads, antlers, such carnage..."

Finding Your Feet

First Two Hours

Arriving By Air

Havana's José Martí International Airport is the main gateway to Cuba, located 15km (9 miles) south of Central Havana, it has three terminals. Most independent travellers will arrive here, but package tourists on "all inclusive" trips may fly to regional airports such as Camagüey, Cienfuegos, Santiago de Cuba, and especially Varadero. In the latter case, all local travel arrangements will have been made in advance by your travel agency. Although there are no international ferry links to Cuba, it is possible to arrange private charters (registration of the vessel in advance is recommended), and cruise ships occasionally call at Havana.

At the Airport

- Items that **cannot legally** be brought into Cuba include narcotics, guns, explosives, pornography, anti-government literature and unprocessed foods. Electronic items, provided they are for personal use and do not have a GPS system, can be brought into Cuba, although you may sometimes be asked to fill in a registration form on arrival.
- It is a good idea to have **luggage** shrink-wrapped for both arrival in and departure from Cuba, to avoid items being "mislaid" from your suitcase.
- There are **shuttle buses** between the various terminals.
- **Lifts** are available in both arrivals and departures, and wheelchair assistance can be arranged.
- On departure, a **tax** of CUC25 for each passenger is payable in cash.

Currency Exchange

- There's really no need to acquire Cuban pesos. The **convertible peso (CUC,** ➤ 171) is the universally accepted form of payment for international visitors, and neither taxi drivers nor hotels will accept anything else (except perhaps US dollars, which as of November 2004 are no longer legal tender). You can obtain convertible pesos at official bureaux de change, called *cadeca*.
- A hefty **10 per cent surcharge** is levied for changing US dollars into CUCs, so avoid bringing cash into the country in this currency. Instead, bring in Canadian dollars or euros, or withdraw cash on arrival at ATMs.
- At all costs, **avoid changing money on the streets**, even if you are offered favourable rates, as the issue of fake notes and scams is common.
- **Credit cards** are accepted in some places – provided the international computer system is up and running, which it often isn't. US-issued and US-bank processed credit cards cannot be used; a fair proportion of British credit cards are issued by US banks, so check before you go.

Tourist Information

Few cities have **official tourist information offices**, and at José Martí International Airport the main purpose of information desks is commercial; the Cuban tourist office does also have some basic information online at www.cubatravel.com.

Getting into Havana

Central Havana is around a 40-minute drive from José Martí International Airport. If you are travelling independently (that is, not on a package), you will need to arrange your own transport. Unless you are extremely patient and on a very tight budget, forget about **buses**, which operate only from the domestic terminal and are extremely crowded and uncomfortable.

Taxis
In town, taxis are efficient and metered, but from the airport it's best to fix a price first; CUC30 is about right for anywhere in downtown Havana. Alternatively, consider arranging a transfer in advance online through a reputable company.

Car Rental
- Several government-owned car rental companies operate desks at José Martí International Airport: **Havanautos** (www.havanautos.com), **Transtur** (www.transtur.cu) and **Rex** (www.rex-rentacar.com). Rex also offers chauffeur-driven vehicles. Most decent hotels also have car rental desks.
- Rental arrangements can be chaotic as there is no central **reservations** system and demand often outstrips supply. Vehicles are often in a poor state of repair, so breakdowns are not uncommon.
- Unless you are very confident, it's best to forego car rental until you are familiar both with **Cuban driving habits** (which are not bad at all) and, more importantly, the layout of sprawling, underlit and ill-signed Havana.
- Rental **rates** vary, but a good standard figure is around CUC50–CUC150 per day including insurance (usually unlimited kilometres), depending on the size of the vehicle. If you're seeking to keep the price down, ask about diesel vehicles – *especial* petrol is expensive.
- Always fill up with fuel when you can as **filling stations** are few and far between and often run short of supplies.

Motorcycle Rental
This option is not generally available in Cuba, though **scooters** may be rented at (and within the precincts of) some tourist resort areas, most notably Varadero. Daily rental prices are around half that of the lowest rate for car rentals – budget about CUC25 a day.

Bicycle Rental
It is **practically impossible** to rent a bicycle in Cuba. If you want to pedal your way around the country, you are advised to bring a bicycle with you.

Getting to Your Hotel
- Havana is a large city with **few road signs** outside tourist zones. Fortunately, most taxi drivers are both helpful and competent in English – though a little Spanish helps to establish friendly relations.
- Choose a **hotel** (perhaps with a fall-back or two) and then simply ask the driver to take you there.
- **Beware** anyone who tells you the hotel of your choice is "full", "closed" or "no good" – they are often simply seeking commissions from their established clients.
- It's usual for flights from Europe (as well as many from Canada) to **arrive in the evening**, often around dusk. Under these circumstances, it's best to head straight to your hotel and settle in, perhaps venturing out later for a short, initial exploration of the area. However, be aware that there are few street lights (and not all of these work) and street crime does exist.

Annoyances
There are **hustlers** (*jineteros*; ➤ 23) and sometimes **prostitutes** (*jineteras*) on just about every side street. Of these, the former are by far the worst, offering you everything from illegal cigars to lobsters, usually preceded by the assurance: "Friend, I don't want anything". Most Cubans are honest, friendly and eager to help you for no reward. However, anyone who forcefully befriends you is intent on monetary gain.

Getting Around

Getting around Cuba isn't hard, but it can be disconcerting and also (especially at night) very dangerous. Not that there's a crime problem – the chances of physical attack are relatively small (although petty theft is endemic) – but hitting an unlit tractor or horse-drawn carriage is a distinct possibility.

Orientation

Road signs off the main tourist routes are virtually non-existent. This really is a serious problem which, hopefully, the government will tackle in the not-too-distant future. There are plenty of signs, of course – but they have nothing to do with road directions and a great deal to do with denunciations of the US and the inevitable victory of socialism.

Driving

- The best way to see Cuba is by **self-drive car**. Several government-owned car rental companies exist, and renting a car is relatively simple – all you need is a credit card and an international driver's licence.
- Bear in mind that, unless it is absolutely necessary, driving **after nightfall** should be avoided at all costs.
- Driving is **on the right**.
- **Seat belts** are compulsory.
- **Speed limits** are applied fairly rigorously, with fines added to your car rental bill. Speed limits are set at 40kph (24.8mph) around schools, 50kph (31mph) in towns, 60kph (37.2mph) on dirt roads, 90kph (55.8mph) on paved highways and 100kph (62mph) on the motorway or *autopista*.
- **Traffic** – motorized traffic – is very light indeed, due to a paucity of vehicles and the high price of fuel.
- Cubans tend to be **careful drivers**, not least because a car is so valuable a commodity (Cubans may not legally own a post-1961 vehicle without permission; the majority are owned by the State) and because spare parts are so hard to come by.
- **Hazards** such as horse-drawn buses, ox carts, farmyard equipment – all unlit at night – and flocks of sheep, goats and cows are potential sources of danger to drivers.
- **Railway tracks**, often unmarked, cut across every road in Cuba from the smallest country lane to the Carretera Central. Many of these are used for harvesting sugar, but even the main tracks for passenger trains can appear unexpectedly – those that cross the *autopista* can be lethal.
- Causing an **accident** resulting in injury or death is a criminal offence in Cuba – drive with utmost caution.

The Autopista

- Cuba has an **extensive road network** amounting to more than 20,000km (12,400 miles) of paved roads, but most are so narrow that even a bicycle can prevent overtaking in the face of oncoming traffic.
- The main arterial route is the *Carretera Central*, built in the 1920s and little upgraded since. There are no drains, and torrential rains can quickly turn the surface into a virtual river.
- In the 1970s, flushed with funds from the Soviet Union, the Castro government began building an *autopista*, or **motorway**, intended to stretch from Pinar del Río in the west to Guantánamo City in the east. About half of it had been completed when the Soviet bloc collapsed in 1990, and today the four-lane motorway is incomplete and badly deteriorated.

- Driving the Cuban *autopista* is a pretty unique experience. There's **virtually no traffic** – this is because there is little fuel available, and few people other than tourists have access to cars or petrol.
- Every entry and exit point, as well as under bridges, is packed with **hitch-hikers** who will wander into the road and flag you down. Try to give lifts wherever possible – the risks are minimal, and this is the only real way for many people to get around. Your memories of the Cubans you meet this way are likely to be one of the highlights of your trip.
- Some **pedestrians** may also block the road to try to sell you strings of garlic or pieces of cheese – strictly illegal private enterprise in socialist Cuba – or just stroll across the six-lane highway from one field to another.

Bus

- *Guaguas,* or buses, serve most cities in Cuba, but services are irregular, overcrowded and generally hot.
- The giant hump-backed buses known locally as *camellos*, or camels, are being replaced by more modern versions, and in Veradaro and Havana hop-on, hop-off, open-top double-decker buses have also been introduced.
- **Long-distance travel** by bus between major tourist destinations is generally fast, efficient and comfortable. It is offered by Víazul (www.viazul.com).
- Local buses, or *camiones*, are really just converted lorries (which are off-limits to tourists) with standing room only.

Train

- Cuba is the only Caribbean country with a functioning rail network. It's not fast, not necessarily on time, and not always comfortable, nor clean, but it is **relatively cheap** and somewhat reliable.
- **Timetables** are likely to change at short notice.
- The rail journey between **Havana and Santiago de Cuba** takes around 13 hours, but leaves only every few days.

Internal Flights

- Cuba has a fairly extensive internal air system linking all major cities with Havana. There are currently **several internal airlines**, but – as so often in socialist Cuba – this does not mean there is a great deal of competition in prices.
- Internal flights still rely heavily on ageing and frankly outdated Soviet aircraft and **reliability and safety** are real concerns.
- Make **reservations** through your hotel or at a local travel agency.

Boats and Ferries

- Several large towns, including Havana, Cienfuegos and Santiago de Cuba, have **local ferries** that shuttle regularly across their ports.
- **Fast passenger catamarans** carry passengers between Surgidero de Batabanó in southern Havana Province and Nueva Gerona on the Isla de la Juventud and make the 100km (62-mile) crossing in around two hours.
- The ageing 500-car-and-passenger ferry, or *barco*, completes the trip between Surgidero de Batabanó in southern Havana Province and Nueva Gerona on the Isla de la Juventud in six hours.

Admission Charges

The cost of admission for museums and places of interest mentioned in the text is indicated by the following price categories:

Inexpensive under CUC2   **Moderate** CUC2–5   **Expensive** over CUC5

Accommodation

Accommodation in Cuba is slowly improving, but still has a long way to go. What's more, the situation is not likely to improve dramatically under the present system, whereby the government maintains complete monopoly on hotels and does everything in its (very considerable) power to restrict competition from legally permitted private room rentals.

Accommodation Agencies

■ The Cuban authorities have organized a number of hotel agencies, of which the largest is **Cubanacán** (www.cubanacan.cu), that administer accommodation nationwide. They look and sound independent and in competition, but they are not. Each operates its own website providing detailed information on all its hotels and permitting reservations by email.

■ The other major government accommodation agencies are **Gaviota** (www. gaviota-grupo.com), **Gran Caribe** (www.gran-caribe.com), **Islazul** (www. islazul.com) and **Habaguanex** (www.habaguanexhotels.com). As a general rule, Gaviota tends to be more upmarket, while Islazul is often the most reasonably priced and has the best bargains. Still, when additional costs, such as breakfast, buffet dinners and parking, are added, it's surprising how similar prices tend to be across the board. Most Cuban hotels are vastly overpriced by international comparison.

■ If you are an independent traveller, a **print-out of any confirmation of reservation** is useful to carry with you on entry at José Martí International Airport in case immigration should ask.

Tourist Hotels

■ The Cuban government owns all hotels in the country, although in **special tourist havens** like Varadero and Cayo Coco many hotels are managed by international companies for a stake of the profit.

■ Since 2008, Cubans are permitted to stay in tourist hotels (although few can afford it), while conversely ordinary tourists are not intended to stay in the **inexpensive peso hotels** available to Cubans.

■ One of the biggest hotel chains in the country is **Islazul** (www.islazul.cu), which operates hotels in 15 different locations in Cuba, many of them listed within this guide.

All-Inclusive Resorts

■ The all-inclusive system is simple – you pay a **fixed price** to your local travel agent for a return flight and a week or two in a resort. This includes a room (usually very comfortable, with facilities such as cable TV), all the food and drink you want in the buffet, restaurants and bars, plus a variety of beach and water activities and evening entertainment.

■ **Amenities** at most resorts include a large area of landscaped grounds, bars, restaurants, swimming pools, gymnasiums, tennis courts and other sports facilities.

■ Generally speaking, the only Cubans permitted on site are those who work or who are staying there. Very often walk-in tourists are not welcome, either. The system is pretty strictly **reserve in advance**.

■ The **major concentrations** of all-inclusives are in Varadero, Cayo Coco and Guadalavaca on the northern (Atlantic) coast, and at Cayo Largo, Playa Ancón, the Jardines de la Reina and Marea del Portillo on the southern (Caribbean) coast.

■ The most positive aspect of the all-inclusive system is that it permits visitors to relax completely within a **private enclave**. The major drawback is that guests see little and learn less about Cuba outside this enclave. With the exception of Varadero, which is within easy striking distance of Matanzas and Cárdenas, most all-in resorts are geographically remote from Cuban population hubs, so that even those who would like to strike out and "see the real Cuba" will find it both difficult and expensive.

Boutique Hotels

There are an increasing number of boutique hotels in Cuba – in Havana and across the country. This trend looks set to gain real momentum over the next few years, which will transform visitors' holiday experiences. The government agency, **Habaguanex** (www.habaguanex.com), is responsible for government-owned boutique hotels, many of which are in historic buildings. Increasingly, foreign investors are appearing on the scene, with companies such as **Esencia** (www.esenciagroup.com) really making their mark by opening a significant number of boutique hotels throughout Cuba.

Joint Enterprises

Since 1990, most Cuban government hotel chains have signed joint management agreements with overseas hotel companies, such as **Accor** (France; www.accorhotels.com), **Iberostar** (Spain; www.iberostar.com) and **Sol Meliá** (Spain; www.solmelia.com). As a consequence, many run-down hotels have been refurbished, and the standard of accommodations in these joint-venture hotels continues to improve on a yearly basis.

Peso Hotels

There are various **inexpensive hotels and boarding houses** accepting non-convertible pesos all over Cuba, but these are intended for Cubans only and it's very difficult, and getting harder, for non-Cubans to stay in such establishments. In any event, most are of abysmal quality and will appeal only to the hardiest budget traveller.

Casas Particulares

- *Casas particulares* are guest houses with **private rooms**. This became legal back in 1993 when the Cuban authorities started to permit limited private enterprise, and it rapidly took off as Cubans all over the country converted their homes into little guest houses.
- They may appeal to you if you wish to gain insights into the lives of Cubans, although conditions vary markedly and you should not expect the amenities you will find in hotels. However, most *casas particulares* are spotless and comfortable with owners who cannot do enough for you.
- *Casas particulares* are distinguished by dark blue **Arrendador Divisa** signs resembling inverted anchors on their front doors.
- Most of these operations do not have their own internet sites owing to the prohibitive cost, but there are a number of general **websites** that offer a booking service, such as www.casaparticularcuba.org.
- *Casas particulares* are **prohibited in resort areas**, such as Varadero and Cayo Coco. However, there are many in Havana and major cities.
- They operate under the weight of onerous taxation and other restrictions, and every year many *casas particulares* are forced to close, so **check the current situation** before you travel.

Prices

The prices given in the listings are for a standard double room per night.
$ under CUC50 $$ CUC50–CUC150 $$$ over CUC150

Food and Drink

Cuba doesn't have one of the world's great culinary traditions, and although the food is tasty, nutritious and filling, cuisine is often bland and many Cubans face severe shortages. Cuban dishes consist mainly of pork and chicken, although there's fish, crab, prawn and lobster in the warm seas all around the island. Just about any vegetable or fruit will grow readily in the fertile soil, but they are usually in short supply.

Tourist restaurants are given priority in the state-run distribution system. Elsewhere, shortages are frequent, and you should get used to hearing *no hay* ("there isn't any") when ordering items off restaurant menus. Frequently, all that is available is a simple ham and cheese sandwich – a *bocadito de jamón y queso*. Also, private sale of food items is restricted to a limited number of farmers' markets *(mercados agropecuarios)*, found in most cities. Between towns, places to buy foodstuffs are virtually non-existent.

Origins of Flavour
Comida criolla (Cuban cuisine) is a combination chiefly of Spanish and Afro-Caribbean cooking, with the addition of some Arabic and Portuguese influences. Rarely spicy, the flavour of most traditional Cuban dishes comes from *sofrito*, a uniquely Cuban blend of garlic, green peppers, oregano, bay leaves and onions.

Local Restaurants
It is possible for the visitor to eat well in Havana – very well in certain locations – and you can get by comfortably in major cities like Cienfuegos, Camagüey and Santiago de Cuba, though good restaurants are few and far between. It's also possible to eat extremely cheaply – ridiculously cheaply, in fact – by resorting to ordinary pesos and joining a queue for **subsidized Cuban food**, though this is almost certainly going to be limited to sub-standard sausage sandwiches, hamburgers or cheese pizzas.

International Restaurants
Fortunately, for visitors, there's no real problem. International-standard restaurants are springing up all over the place in Havana and the major resorts, such as Varadero, Cayo Coco, Cayo Largo and Guardalavaca. There are a few good *criollo* restaurants supplied with quality provisions in major cultural hubs, such as Trinidad, Remedios, Santiago de Cuba and Camagüey, too. Elsewhere it's a different story, and visitors seeking a meal in small provincial towns off the beaten track are likely to find their choice limited to pizzas, hamburgers and spaghetti.

Paladares
In general, by far the best meals are to be had in **private restaurants**, which flourished during the 1990s when Castro allowed limited private enterprise. People were permitted to serve meals in their homes but not to employ staff – it had to be a family-run operation. Unfortunately, *paladares* are now being closed down in many cities. Havana, though, is still blessed with several excellent *paladares*.

What to Eat
- Most Cubans like **meat** – and lots of it. Fried and grilled chicken, pork and grilled fish are enduringly popular. Beef is a rarity served only in tourist restaurants, as is fresh **seafood**, such as squid, octopus, prawns and

lobster. The quality of the pork, in particular, is generally excellent and on weekends it is not unusual to see pigs being roasted on the spit for a family party.

■ Fresh vegetables are rare – **canned vegetables** are the norm. **Salad** is available on most menus, but it's likely to consist of sliced cucumber or cold green beans. Cuban cuisine tends to be as macho as its culture – most people are voracious meat-eaters, although Cubans are highly educated about the health benefits of fruit and vegetables.

■ Havana and a few other cities have at least one **vegetarian** restaurant, and the numbers seem to be increasing.

■ **Accompaniments** to meat and seafood are usually fried potatoes, yucca cooked with garlic, or rice and pulses. The latter comes in two varieties: *Moros y Cristianos* (Muslims and Christians) in the west and middle of the country – or black beans and white rice, a tradition which must go back to the days of battle between Christians and Muslims in Spain; or *congrí*, a succulent mix of white rice and red kidney beans, in the east.

La Cocina Baracoa
Cuba is unusual in not having – with one notable exception – any distinctive **regional cuisines**. Only Baracoa (► 138–139), in the far east of the country, claims this distinction. There, rice is cooked in coconut milk and more spices are used than in the rest of the country, including annatto seeds to turn rice yellow, as well as *tamales* made of mashed plantains and minced pork rather than the usual boiled corn and minced pork.

Eating in Hotels
Dining in Cuba can be very good for those staying in **all-inclusive resorts** in places such as Varadero and Cayo Coco, although at some all-inclusive hotels the cuisine, usually in the form of buffets, falls far short of most people's expectations. If you don't fancy all-inclusive accommodation but would like to eat at your hotel, bear in mind that it's almost impossible to find a hotel that provides three meals a day but isn't all-inclusive.

What to Drink
■ It's best to **avoid tap water** and buy the readily available bottled varieties – whether still or sparkling.

■ **Beer** is good and on sale everywhere, though usually in bottles or cans rather than on tap. Motorized beer dispensers for the masses serve a lesser quality but ludicrously cheap local beer called *claro*.

■ There is a wide choice of **soft drinks**.

■ **Rum** (► 9–10) is ubiquitous, and is the staple of every Cuban cocktail.

■ **Wine** is available at most of the better restaurants in Havana and other big cities.

Tipping
Even though many restaurants add on a service charge, waiting staff will see little, or any, of this. Most people who work in Cuba are on starvation wages of less than a dollar a day. A tip to your waiter (as well as room cleaner, driver, etc.) goes a long way towards feeding a family in Cuba.

Restaurant Prices
Prices in this book are based on the amount you should expect to pay per person for a two-course meal, excluding drinks and service charges.
$ under CUC10 $$ CUC10–CUC25 $$$ over CUC25

Shopping

Cuba isn't really a shopper's paradise. Nevertheless, there are things to buy in Cuba, and Havana is certainly the best place in the country to go shopping. Cuba's art scene is incredibly vibrant and there are tremendous bargains to be had in artwork and crafts, while Cuban cigars, coffee and rums are must-buys that rank among the best in the world.

Souvenirs

- **Shops at large hotels** sell a variety of souvenirs, ranging from dolls to maracas, leatherwork, woodcarvings and other assorted knick-knacks. Much of this is very high quality.
- Enduringly popular, the image of Ernesto "Che" Guevara decorates everything from T-shirts to plates and wooden plaques, and there is a wealth of books by or about the revolutionary hero. It's also possible to buy **Che Guevara** posters, postcards and characteristic black berets with the red star of communism on the front.
- Handcrafted **leather** sandals, cowboy boots and belts are good buys, as are **straw hats** and embroidered *guayabera* **shirts**, **lace** blouses and tablecloths.
- **Street markets** are the best places to buy, although **state-run art galleries** have a virtual monopoly on the highest-quality creations.
- Casas del Habano cigar stores are found in virtually every city and are the best places to buy **cigars**. Avoid buying cigars on the street.

Music

Cuban music (➤ 6–8) is one of the island's marvels. In a country that seemingly never stops dancing, a wide range of CDs is available for sale and at prices equivalent to the US or Europe. Music CDs are sold in shops and on street corners, and musicians performing in bars and hotels will often approach you with recordings of their own work. Definitely a high point in the Cuban shopping scene.

Art

Perhaps because it's clearly a cultural activity, the state doesn't interfere too much in the painting and drawing scene. All over the island, but especially in La Habana Vieja and at major tourist attractions, paintings of all kinds – but especially modern art Cuban-style – are for sale at free markets. There are some real bargains to be had, and haggling over the price is an accepted norm, within reason.

Imported Goods

It's hard to find everyday things like batteries, medicines, even toothpaste and shampoo – except at special government stores, which charge highly inflated prices. It's best to bring your own supplies with you. Even paper and pens can be hard to find so bring some for yourself, but also for gifts for your hosts or people you meet on your trip. A few boutiques in Havana and tourist resorts sell imported clothing. Elsewhere, boutiques of international standard are virtually non-existent, and duty-free shops are limited.

Preserving Nature

Despite its revolutionary nature, the Cuban government doesn't seem to have grasped the need to protect the island's natural environment. This means that souvenirs are available made from wild plants, animal parts, stuffed birds, sea shells, coral and even shell from endangered marine turtles. All in all, it's best to stay well away from souvenirs of this kind.

Entertainment

Cubans are a fun-loving people. Festivals are enduringly popular – especially the Santiago de Cuba carnival. There is live jazz and salsa, and virtually every town has a Las Vegas-style *cabaret espectáculo* and a *casa de trova* traditional music venue. The latest films from the US and Latin America are watched by enthusiastic audiences. Beach activities include windsurfing and snorkelling. Baseball is the most popular sport, though Cubans excel at boxing (➤ 26–27).

Cuba has a wide choice of entertainment options, of which the best known are those designed specifically for well-heeled, international visitors, such as the Tropicana nightclub. More authentic choices include folk music, jazz clubs, dancing, cabaret shows, discos, drama, ballet, movies and classical music recitals. One of the joys of Cuba is the way in which people make their own fun at impromptu house and street parties, where foreign visitors are always made welcome. For information about **upcoming events**, rely on the grapevine or the regularly updated cultural listings on the *Cuba Absolutely* website (www.cubaabsolutely.com), which also offers the facility to buy tickets for events.

Nightlife

- Ask for the local *casa de trova* in almost any Cuban town and you will be directed to a sort of musical club where Cubans get together to play music and sing *boleros,* son and other traditional music forms, especially at weekends.
- There are **nightclubs** in many all-inclusive resorts and at most large hotels, where Cuba's finest salsa bands often perform. Cubans have their own night scene with disco dancing and low-priced nightclubs. The latter can sometimes be a bit basic by international standards, but visitors are invariably made most welcome.
- In a continuation from the pre-revolutionary 1940s and 50s, Cuba has a tradition of **gala-style cabarets** with big bands and leggy showgirls barely dressed in elaborate costumes and astonishing head-dresses. Havana, Santiago de Cuba and Varadero are the main venues for this kind of entertainment, although such sensual cabarets are a staple of local nightlife nationwide. Such venues usually have discos after the show.
- There are plenty of **bars and drinking spots** all over Cuba, most extremely run-down and aimed primarily at the local clientele. Visiting one is a good way to meet the locals, however, and you may even have trouble paying for that shot of rum – Cubans are a generous bunch, and usually only too happy to make your acquaintance. More upmarket bars are common in tourist hot-spots like Havana and Varadero. Most tourist bars host live music regularly.

Theatre and Performance Arts

- All of Cuba's provincial capitals boast **theatres** where plays (generally in Spanish) are presented on a regular basis.
- **Children's theatre** – a kind of Caribbean pantomime – is enduringly popular, as are puppet shows.
- Cuba prides itself on being a cultured country, and the communist authorities have long sought to promote classical music and ballet. **Classical music** is performed at the *Casa de la Cultura*, found in every major Cuban town, and at various theatres in Havana and major cities.
- Watch the entertainments listings for performances by the **Ballet Nacional de Cuba** (➤ 60).

Cinema and Funfairs

- Cuban **cinemas** are pretty run-down and behind the times in the range of Hollywood and home-grown movies they show. On the other hand they are cheap and friendly.
- Travelling **funfairs** are popular with the locals, but your individual safety concerns should be heeded as it will be apparent that the age of the machines and standard of maintenance of funfair rides leaves much to be desired.

Entertainment in All-inclusive Resorts

The all-inclusive resorts make a big effort to ensure their guests have plenty of **activities** to choose from, both by day and by night. Daytime activities include aerobics in and around the pool, dance lessons, beach volleyball and football, windsurfing, scuba-diving – even (at Varadero) sky-diving. At night, there are **shows** featuring singing and dancing, with audience participation actively encouraged.

Sports

- **Baseball** is Cuba's most popular sport (➤ 27), and if you have the opportunity it's well worth going along to a game, although stadiums are not up to the standards of North America or Europe. Cubans are passionate about baseball – their enthusiasm is part of the fun.
- Cuba's many unspoiled beaches offer plenty of opportunities for **watersports**. Try parasailing or windsurfing; go snorkelling or diving around coral reefs; join a deep-sea fishing trip or enjoy sailing, surfing or just plain swimming in the warm waters of the Caribbean.
- **Adventure sports** are not yet a big draw in Cuba, but the future for trekking, rock climbing and bicycling looks promising – it's just a question of time.
- For **specialist holidays**, such as fishing, bird-watching, watersports or adventure sports, you are advised to make arrangements with an international operator before arrival, although day tours can be arranged on the ground.
- **Bird watching** is very popular in Cuba and a well-established activity, with many indigenous species to see.

Festivals

- **Religion** is making a comeback in post-Soviet Cuba, and both the major Christian festivals (especially Easter) and local Santería festivals are celebrated with increasing openness.
- For five days every February, Havana is the setting for a **cigar festival** (www.festivaldelhabano.com), which celebrates one of the country's most famous exports with gusto.
- Fishing fanatics won't want to miss the long-standing **Ernest Hemingway International Marlin Fishing Tournament** that takes place every June at Marina Hemingway.
- Cuba's most famous festival is the Santiago de Cuba **Carnival**, held in the eastern capital on 25–27 July every year, though the celebrations may spill over on either side. A similar but less authentic carnival is held in Havana in August, for which locals rehearse every week at *comparsas* or carnival dance schools.
- In December, the **Havana jazz festival** (www.jazzcuba.com) attracts world-class musicians as well as visitors from all over the world.
- The **Festival of New Latin American Cinema**, held every December in cinemas across the country, focuses on Spanish language films (with subtitles). It usually draws a sprinkling of Hollywood stars.

Havana

Getting Your Bearings

Most visitors to Cuba will explore Havana, the country's vibrant but somewhat decaying capital. This sprawling metropolis shakes and sizzles with excitement. Although both Vedado, in the west, and Centro have their share of modern high-rise buildings, it's La Habana Vieja – Old Havana, in the east – which is the heart of the city and the one of most important Spanish colonial hubs in the whole of Latin America.

Havana is two cities. By day modern, hop-on, hop-off, open-top double-decker buses vie for space on the pot-holed streets with 50-year-old American jalopies. There's music in the air, and an astonishing range of architectural styles, from colonial Spanish to early 20th-century American, to delight the eye. To the north, the waves of the Straits of Florida lap or lash against the sea walls. Everywhere there are national monuments, as well as some excellent museums.

By night, Havana is another world, dimly lit and slightly unnerving. However, there's a policeman on virtually every corner in tourist areas, and once you get used to the cigar-hustlers and occasional prostitutes – most of whom will respond to a simple "*no me molestes!*" by apologizing and disappearing – there is little to worry about. However, as in any major city, it makes sense to take reasonable precautions, particularly with valuables.

Previous page: Dusk falls over Havana

Below: Plaza Vieja, once the slave market, has been restored

In Three Days

If you're not quite sure where to begin your travels, this itinerary recommends three practical and enjoyable days out in Havana, taking in some of the best places to see using the Getting Your Bearings map on the previous page. For more information, see the main entries.

Day 1

Morning

Explore **3 La Habana Vieja** (➤ 54–56) by walking the streets of the old town (Havana walk, ➤ 156–158), visiting at least two of the main squares – Plaza de Armas and **7 Plaza de la Catedral** (above; ➤ 59–60). Lunch at the legendary La Bodeguita del Medio (➤ 67), an old haunt of Hemingway, which is admittedly touristy but should not be missed.

Afternoon

Continue your exploration of La Habana Vieja, making sure you visit Plaza de San Francisco and Plaza Vieja. Stop for a well-deserved sundowner at **Taberna de la Muralla** (➤ 68) on Plaza Vieja and stroll back along **8 Calle Obispo** (➤ 60).

Evening

Have an early dinner at the excellent **Restaurant Santo Ángel** (➤ 68), on Plaza Vieja, then head out to the **Malecón** (➤ 50–51) for an evening stroll starting at the Castillo de San Salvador de la Punta and finishing at Torreón de San Lázaro.

Day 2

Morning
Take a taxi to visit Havana's two great citadels, **4 El Morro and La Cabaña** (➤ 57–58). Take another taxi back to the **2 Museo de la Revolución** (right; ➤ 52–53), where you can spend an hour absorbing Cuba's recent history. Then admire the fabulous art collection of the **6 Museo Nacional de Bellas Artes** (➤ 59) before lunch in the Moorish Restaurante Anacaona ($) in the Hotel Saratoga (➤ 65; daily 12–10:45).

Afternoon
Stroll around **9 Parque Central** (➤ 60), taking in the Capitolio and Partagás cigar factory (➤ 60–61), then stroll south down shady **5 El Prado** (➤ 59).

Evening
Have dinner at Cocina de Lilliam (➤ 66), probably the best restaurant in Havana – make sure to book a table in advance. End the evening at La Casa de La Música (➤ 71).

Day 3

Morning
Take a taxi or rent a car for the day and drive southeast to the **15 Museo Hemingway** (below; ➤ 63) in the sleepy suburban village of San Francisco de Paula. Then continue to the small fishing village of **16 Cojímar** (➤ 63) for a seafood lunch at Hemingway's old hangout, the Restaurante La Terraza (➤ 68).

Afternoon
Return to Havana and the district of Vedado, stopping to visit the **13 Plaza de la Revolución** (➤ 62), the **12 Cementerio de Colón** (➤ 61–62), and Castro's tribute to The Beatles, **11 Parque John Lennon** (➤ 61).

Evening
Tonight tuck into a traditional Cuban meal of roast chicken at El Aljibe (➤ 66), one of Havana's best *criollo* restaurants, before enjoying the Tropicana (➤ 72) cabaret.

⓿ Malecón

Havana's most famous thoroughfare is the celebrated Malecón, also known as Avenida Antonio Maceo, which runs the length of the capital's considerable seafront with the *Estrecho de la Florida* (Straits of Florida). By day and night, the Malecón is Havana's epicentre of social life, and just about everyone comes to stroll, sit on the sea wall, fish, swim or gossip.

The Malecón in its present form was constructed under the US military administration in 1901. An old Spanish fort, **Castillo de San Salvador de la Punta**, in La Habana Vieja, marks the eastern end. From here it runs westwards for 8km (5 miles) through Central Havana and Vedado to **Castillo de la Chorrera**, another small Spanish fortress marking the boundary between Vedado and Miramar districts.

The eastern end of the Malecón has fine views of the great fortress of El Morro (➤ 57–58), which guards the entrance to Havana Harbour. In this area, during the colonial era, large tanks for bathing or washing were cut into the solid rock just offshore. Walking west, the once grand apartment houses of Central Havana line the route as far as the Monumento Antonio Maceo, dedicated to the memory of the great independence fighter. Close by, the Torreón de San Lázaro was once a Spanish watchtower.

Monument to the Maine

About 1.5km (0.9 miles) farther west, the Hotel Nacional dominates the skyline. Nearby is the **Monumento al Maine**, originally built to honour the victims of the mysterious explosion which sank the USS *Maine* in 1898 and provided an excuse for the Spanish-American War later the same year. The monument, complete with cannons from the *Maine* recovered from the bay, was once topped by an American eagle, but today bears the inscription (in Spanish, on the marble tablet in front) "To the victims of the *Maine* who were sacrificed by voracious imperialism in its desire to seize Cuba."

Castillo de San Salvador stands at the eastern end of the Malecón

The Malecón is a busy thoroughfare at night

Ten minutes' walk west of the Maine Monument is the impressive **Monumento Calixto García**, dedicated to another great revolutionary hero. The monument features 24 bronze plaques detailing García's 30-year struggle in the late 19th century against the Spanish. One mile farther west rises the modernist Hotel Riviera (➤ 65), built by mobster Meyer Lansky (➤ 18–19) on the eve of the Revolution.

TAKING A BREAK

For a prime view both ways along the Malecón, try the Hotel Nacional (➤ 64). This 1930s art deco landmark serves pretty good food and also permits non-guests dining here to use the hotel's large outdoor pool.

➕ 184 B4 ✉ Avenida Antonio de Maceo

MALECÓN: INSIDE INFO

Top tips If exploring the Malecón on foot **stick to the northern sidewalk**, next to the sea. Driving is another matter; from east to west you see the waterfront, but from west to east, you'll be farther inland, and will see much less of the shore. It's probably best to drive the Malecón both ways, starting and finishing at the eastern end.

■ **Watch out for hustlers** at all times, prostitutes (who can be pushy at night), and – more dangerous and harder to avoid than either of the former – deep pot-holes at places in the badly eroded pavement.

■ During bad weather and the hurricane season in September, **huge waves** can batter the sea wall, drenching the Malecón and anybody walking along it.

2 Museo de la Revolución

Fittingly, the Museum of the Revolution is housed in the former palace of Cuban dictator Fulgencio Batista (➤ 15, 19), overthrown by Fidel Castro (➤ 15, 20–22) in 1959. The building was constructed between 1913 and 1920 in grand neoclassical style, and the interior was decorated by Tiffany's of New York. It is a beautiful building, and is worth a visit for the eclectic architecture as much as for the revolutionary artefacts gathered both within and round about.

Part of the museum is devoted to the revolutionary exploits of Cuban nationalists during the Wars of Independence, and the grand stairway is dominated by a bust of José Martí, the father of the nation, as well as by a Cuban flag. The exhibits are laid out on three floors connected by a monumental marble stairway rising to an **impressive dome** patterned with fine ceramic tiles. Immediately beneath this is a heroic but less artistically accomplished mural of Cuban independence fighters battling the Spanish in the Wars of Independence. Another impressive architectural feature is the **Salón de los**

A stunning ceiling fresco covers the Salón de los Espejos

An elegant corridor in the former presidential palace

Espejos (Room of Mirrors), a great reception room on the first floor leading to three balconies from which Batista – and the Cuban presidents and dictators who preceded him – used to address the people.

Also of historical merit and unrelated to the revolutionary events is the **Baluarte del Ángel**, a surviving watchtower from the old city wall, now somewhat overshadowed by the SAU-100 Soviet tank parked next to it. This vehicle was supposedly used by Fidel Castro in his successful defeat of the Bay of Pigs invasion in 1961.

Revolutionary History

Most of the exhibits within the museum relate directly to the Cuban Revolution of 1959 and especially to the heroism of Camilo Cienfuegos, Ernesto "Che" Guevara (➤ 20–22)and Fidel Castro. A Fidel personality cult is ubiquitous throughout Cuba and here, at the museum, Fidel certainly features. The exhibits give a detailed chronological record of the events leading to the overthrow of Batista, from the initial attack on the Moncada Barracks in 1953 (➤ 19, 21), the battles with the US, plus revolutionary achievements, through to recent times. There is an almost sanctified feel to the salons exhibiting the guns, bombs, bloodstained uniforms, detailed military maps and pictures of martyrs; curators tend to follow visitors around the museum in case they show insufficient respect or even touch something.

Outside is the equally hallowed **Granma Memorial** displaying the yacht *Granma*, used by Fidel and his revolutionaries to land in Oriente in 1956. It's housed in a glass-walled building. Scattered around are missiles, military aircraft plus other vehicles used in the revolution, including a bus that carried munitions and a bulldozer converted to become a tank. It's under permanent military guard, and once again the atmosphere is reverential.

TAKING A BREAK

Head east into La Habana Vieja for *criollo* fare and *mojitos* at Hemingway's old hangout, **La Bodeguita del Medio** (➤ 67), just a short stroll away on Calle Empedrado.

➕ 185 E4 ✉ Calle Refugio 1, between Agramonte and Avenida de las Misiones ☎ (7) 862-4091 ⏱ Daily 10–5 💲 Moderate

MUSEO DE LA REVOLUCIÓN: INSIDE INFO

Don't miss El Rincón de los Cretinos (Cretin's Corner), near the gift shop, displays life-sized caricatures of politicians particularly despised or hated by the Cuban Revolution.

❸ La Habana Vieja

La Habana Vieja (Old Havana) is the most important and exciting attraction in all Cuba. It was declared a National Monument in 1977, and a UNESCO World Heritage Site in 1982, but restoration of this, the most significant centre of Spain's colonial heritage in all the Americas, has been painfully slow. At present, the heart of La Habana Vieja is already sufficiently restored to be truly wonderful. The south, a slum area with few sights of interest, requires caution.

Vibrant hues in 16th-century Plaza Vieja

Old Havana is dominated by four main squares linked by a narrow grid of cross-streets that are gradually being cobbled and restored. They are all within easy walking distance of each other. It is best to start in the **Plaza de Armas**, which dates from 1582 and is the oldest square in the city. Approached from Central Havana by Calle Obispo (➤ 60), this shady square has been almost completely restored and is home to fine colonial buildings, several good restaurants and a lively second-hand book market.

On the northeast side of the square is the **Castillo de la Real Fuerza**, the oldest colonial fortress in the New World. The weathervane on top of the west tower is a female figure, La Giraldilla, which has become the symbol of Havana. This is a replica – the original, dating from 1632, is in the baroque **Museo de la Ciudad** on the west side of Plaza de Armas in the former governor's palace, the Palacio de los Capitanes Generales. In the heart of the square is a statue of national hero Carlos Manuel de Céspedes (➤ 14, 15). Often there is live music in the square, with women dancing to Afro-Cuban rhythms – expect to pay if you want to take pictures. The city's most spectacular square, Plaza de la Catedral (➤ 59–60), is two blocks northwest.

Other Squares

About 200m (220 yards) to the south is the **Plaza de San Francisco**, with some of the most attractive colonial houses in Old Havana and the **Iglesia y Convento de San Francisco de Asís**, no longer a church but a concert hall and museum of religious art. The church tower, at 36m (118 feet), is the tallest in Havana. A white marble fountain, the Fuente de los Leones (Fountain of Lions), dominates the heart of the square.

On the south side of the Iglesia San Francisco is Parque Humboldt, named after the German explorer Alexander von Humboldt. His house, the **Casa Alejandro von Humboldt**, exhibits displays of his contribution to the cataloguing of Cuba's fauna and flora in the 19th century. The nearby **Museo del Ron** (Museum of Rum) is also worth a visit.

Just 100m (110 yards) southwest of the Plaza de San Francisco is the third of Old Havana's distinguished squares, **Plaza Vieja**, dating from the mid-16th century and once the capital's main slave market. This magnificent square has been restored, with many of the once-dilapidated buildings transformed into boutiques and restaurants, and the long-defunct fountain brought back to its former glory. On the south of the square, the **Casa de los Condes de Jaruco** has a covered gallery dating from the 1730s with art galleries and craft shops. On the plaza's northeast corner, the **Cámara Oscura** – atop the Edificio Gómez Villa – projects a revolving real-time image of the city at 30x-magnification.

Narrow Back Streets

In addition to the four main squares, virtually every narrow street in Old Havana is resplendent with architectural gems reflecting Cuba's Hispanic colonial past. Two impressive examples are the parallel north–south Calle Oficios and Calle Mercaderes, linking Plaza de Armas with Plaza Vieja. Not to be missed along Mercaderes are the **Maqueta de la Habana**, a scale model of the old city; the **Casa de África**, celebrating Afro-Cuban culture; and, across the street, the **Casa de la Obrapía**, with spectacular baroque features. It's best just to wander these back streets, which are very safe – you'll find a policeman on almost every corner.

The southern half of Habana Vieja is the city's ancient ecclesiastical quarter, with several churches and convents of note. Visit the **Iglesia y Convento de Belén**; the **Iglesia y Convento de Santa Clara de Asís**; and **Iglesia Parroquial del Espíritu Santo**.

TAKING A BREAK

Try the Taberna de la Muralla (► 68) on Plaza Vieja, a tastefully decorated colonial period pub with a microbrewery.

Plaza de Armas
✚ 185 F4

Castillo de la Real Fuerza
✚ 185 F4 ✉ O'Reilly 2 ☎ (7) 861 6130 ⏲ Tue–Sun 9:30–5:30 💷 Inexpensive

Museo de la Ciudad
✚ 185 F4 ✉ Tacón 1 ☎ (7) 861 5001 ⏲ Tue–Sun 9:30–5:30 💷 Inexpensive

Plaza de la Catedral
✚ 185 F4

A restored house in a narrow Old Havana street

Iglesia y Convento de San Francisco de Asís
✚ 185 F4 ✉ Calle Oficios
☎ (7) 862-9683 ⏰ Daily 9–5:30
💷 Inexpensive

Casa Alejandro von Humboldt
✚ 185 F3 ✉ Calle Oficios 254
☎ (7) 863-9850 ⏰ Tue–Sun 9:30–6

Museo del Ron
✚ 185 F4 ✉ San Pedro 262
☎ (7) 861 8051 ⏰ Mon–Thu 9–5, Fri–Sun 9–4 💷 Expensive

Plaza Vieja
✚ 185 F4

Casa de los Condes de Jaruco
✚ 185 F4 ✉ Muralla No 107
☎ (7) 861 8544 ⏰ Mon–Fri 10–5, Sat 10–2 💷 Free

Cámara Oscura
✚ 185 F4 ✉ Plaza Vieja ⏰ Daily 9:30–7 💷 Inexpensive

Casa de África
✚ 185 F4 ✉ Obrapía 157
☎ (7) 861 5798 ⏰ Tue–Sat 9:30–5, Sun 10–12 💷 Inexpensive

Casa de la Obrapía
✚ 185 F4 ✉ Calle Obrapia 158
☎ (7) 861 3097 ⏰ Mon–Thu 9–5:30, Fri–Sat 9–4, Sun 10–4 💷 Free

Iglesia y Convento de Belén
✚ 185 E3 ✉ Calle Compostela
☎ (7) 860-3150 ⏰ Irregular hours 💷 Inexpensive

Iglesia y Convento de Santa Clara de Asís
✚ 185 F4 ✉ Cuba 610
☎ (7) 866 9327 ⏰ Mon–Fri 9–4 💷 Inexpensive

Iglesia Parroquial del Espíritu Santo
✚ 185 F3 ✉ Acosta 161
☎ (7) 862 3410 ⏰ Mon–Fri 9–4 💷 Inexpensive

LA HAVANA VIEJA: INSIDE INFO

Top tips Take it easy – Old Havana isn't for rushing. Fortunately, most of the streets are narrow and therefore shaded. Stop for a cool drink in any or all of the four squares and enjoy the **musical ambience** and incredible street life.

■ **Visit the art and crafts market** at the junction of Calle Tacón and Calle Empedrado, where there's lots of vibrant styles and creative works to buy.

■ **Casa de los Árabes**, at Calle Oficios 16, is a small museum (Tue–Sat 9–4:30, Sun 9–1, inexpensive) that celebrates Arab and Islamic culture in Cuba.

4 El Morro and La Cabaña

Two castles, Castillo de los Tres Santos Reyes del Morro (El Morro) and Fortaleza de San Carlos de la Cabaña (La Cabaña) dominate the narrow entrance to the Bahía de la Habana and Havana Harbour. Together they form the single largest Spanish military complex in the Americas, reinforcing Havana's position as the most important repository of Spain's colonial legacy in the New World.

El Morro, at the northern entrance to the bay, was constructed between 1560 and 1630. It's a massive stone fortress on a sheer limestone headland, which dominates the view east from the Malecón (➤ 50–51) and with its 3m-thick (10-foot) walls must once have seemed all but impregnable. Nevertheless, it was taken by storm by the English in 1762 and held for 11 months. When they eventually withdrew, the Spanish determined to strengthen the defences of the capital by building the even more massive La Cabaña slightly to the south. On being informed of the huge size of this fortress, King Carlos II of Spain is said to have tried to see it through a telescope, commenting jokingly that because of its massive cost it must surely be visible from Madrid.

The lighthouse at Castillo de los Tres Santos Reyes del Morro

Today, El Morro is visited mainly because of the fantastic views it offers across Havana. These are best enjoyed from on top of the lighthouse (*faro*), which was added in 1844. Guarding the bay below is the impressive **Baluarte de los**

Doce Apóstoles (Battery of the Twelve Apostles), named after the 12 cannons mounted there since the days of the Spanish-American War. The former ammunition store is now a small bar, **El Polvorín** (The Powder House; see below).

A Powerful Fortress

La Cabaña is grander and more powerful than El Morro – in fact, it is the largest castle in the Americas and offers stupendous views west across La Habana Vieja and beyond. Built between 1763 and 1774 – it was started just months after the troublesome English departed El Morro – La Cabaña covers 10ha (25 acres). Its stone ramparts are an impressive 12m (40ft) thick in some parts, and the fortress has never been taken in battle. Today restored, with cobbled streets and rows of buildings sheltering behind the mighty ramparts, it houses the **Museo de Fortificaciones y Armas** and the **Museo de Che**, in a structure that served as Che Guevara's headquarters after the Revolution.

A cannon on the ramparts of La Cabaña

A cannon is fired at La Cabaña every night at 9pm by soldiers dressed in colonial military uniform (they are present by day also). It's wise to get there early for a good viewpoint.

TAKING A BREAK

There's the small **El Polvorin** (The Powder House, daily 12–12, $$) bar at El Morro, in the former ammunition store, but much more satisfying is the **Restaurante La Divina Pastora** (Carretera de la Cabana, tel: (7) 860 8341, daily 12–11, $$) at La Cabaña, offering tasty fresh seafood. The restaurant also has live music and an Afro-Cuban show.

El Morro
➕ 185 E5 ✉ Parque Histórico Militar Morro-Cabaña ☎ (7) 863-7941
🕐 Daily 8–8 💵 Moderate

La Cabaña
➕ 185 F5 ✉ Carretera de la Cabaña, Habana del Este ☎ (7) 862-0671
🕐 Daily 8am–10pm 💵 Expensive (includes admission to both museums)

EL MORRO & LA CABAÑA: INSIDE INFO

Top tips Most visitors content themselves with a visit to El Morro. This is a mistake as La Cabaña is the more interesting of the two and – especially during the mornings – much less crowded with tour buses.
■ Climb **El Morro's lighthouse** for the best views of the city.

At Your Leisure

5 El Prado

North of Parque Central, a major boulevard, Paseo de Martí – better known as El Prado – runs towards the Malecón (➤ 50–51). Dating from the late 18th century, it was once home to Havana's richest and most powerful families, and this is certainly reflected in the ornate architecture. By the beginning of the 20th century, the area was already in serious decline, and much of the Prado had become a red light area, with scantily dressed girls standing on the elaborately decorated balconies in order to lure in customers.

Today, the Prado is gradually being restored. A long, tree-shaded central walk ornamented with marble lions and statues of some national heroes enhances the beauty of the colonial architecture.

➕ 186 E5 ✉ Between La Punta Fort and Parque Central

6 Museo Nacional de Bellas Artes

Havana's Museum of Fine Arts is housed in two separate buildings. The first, a beautiful modernist structure immediately south of the Museo de la Revolución (➤ 52–53), displays works by Cuban artists, from early colonial days to contemporary masters such as Wilfredo Lam. The baroque former Supreme Court building, on the east side of Parque Central, exhibits international works on five floors, with such masters as Gainsborough, Goya and Velázquez represented. It also houses Egyptian, Greek and Roman antiquities.

➕ 185 E4 ✉ Calle San Rafael, between Zulueta and Monserrate ☎ (7) 863-9484; www.museonacional.cult.cu 🕓 Tue–Sat 10–6, Sun 10–2 💰 Moderate

7 Plaza de la Catedral

Perhaps the most delightful of Old Havana's squares, this cobbled open

The baroque cathedral dominates charming Plaza de la Catedral

area (pedestrians only) is surrounded by fine buildings and home to the most vibrant of all La Habana Vieja's performance artists. They range from Santería priestesses to sharp-suited dancers to flower girls – all will want payment to photograph them.

The splendid baroque Catedral de la Habana, dating from 1777, dominates the square. The great, brass-bound wooden doors are particularly impressive – locals rap them for good luck at New Year. Other fine buildings include the Casa del Marqués de Arcos, now an art gallery, and the Casa de Lombillo (1741), with an exhibition on the old city's restoration. Directly opposite the cathedral is the Casa del Conde de Casa Bayona (1720), a fine colonial building that contains the Museo de Arte Colonial.

✚ 185 F4 ✉ La Habana Vieja

Catedral de la Habana
◉ Mon–Sat 10–4, Sun 9–12 📋 Free

Museo de Arte Colonial
✉ San Ignacio 61 ☎ (7) 862 6640 ◉ Daily 9–6 📋 Inexpensive

Hotel Ambos Mundos in Calle Obispo

8 Calle Obispo

"Bishop's Street", frequented by the city's ecclesiastics in the 18th century, is perhaps the most famous street in La Habana Vieja. It was the first to be restored after the Old City became a UNESCO World Heritage Site, and has now been cobbled and made into a pedestrian-only zone. Today, it's a great place to sit at one of the street-side cafés or bistros, enjoying a drink and watching the world go by. Or you can visit art galleries or browse shops selling souvenirs.

Walking east down Calle Obispo, look out for the Banco Nacional de Cuba at the junction with Calle Cuba, the Hotel Florida with its fine interior courtyard, the Museo Numismático (Coin Museum) and a wonderful old pharmacy, the Farmacia y Droguería Taquechel – note the skeleton in a glass case visible through the window. At the eastern end of Obispo, at the junction with Mercaderes, is the Hotel Ambos Mundos (➤ 64), where Ernest Hemingway lived for some years in the 1930s and wrote *For Whom The Bell Tolls*. For a small fee, you can visit his room, No 511.

✚ 185 E4 ✉ La Habana Vieja

Museo Numismático
✉ Calle Obispo, between Cuba and Aguiar ☎ (7) 861-5811 ◉ Tue–Sat 9–4:45, Sun 9–1 📋 Inexpensive

9 Parque Central

Parque Central divides La Habana Vieja from Centro and has some very distinguished architecture, including the Hotel Inglaterra, built in 1875, with a fine, neo-baroque facade. Immediately to the south is the splendid Gran Teatro, a fabulously ornate building dating from 1837. It has several auditoria and both the National Ballet of Cuba and the State Opera perform here. In the square opposite, surrounded by fine royal palms, is a white marble statue of national hero José Martí (➤ 15).

Immediately south of Parque Central is the vast and grandiose El Capitolio, the former Congressional building, erected in the 1920s and styled on the Capitol in Washington DC. Immediately behind (to the west) of the Capitolio, don't miss the fine Fábrica de Tabacos Partagás building; this famous cigar factory offers guided tours.

🕂 185 E4 ⊠ El Capitolio ☎ (7) 861-5519 🕓 Daily 9–7 🎫 Moderate

Fábrica de Tabacos Partagás
⊠ Calle Industria 520 🕓 Mon–Sat 9–5 🎫 Expensive

🔟 Barrio Chino

Large numbers of Chinese labourers came to Cuba around 1850; most came to work in the sugar fields and build railways. A second wave arrived in the 1870s, fleeing anti-Chinese sentiment and legislation in California. Finally, a third wave took refuge here after the overthrow of the Qing Dynasty in 1911. By the beginning of the 20th century, the ethnic Chinese population of Cuba had reached 50,000, and Havana's Chinatown, or Barrio Chino, was the largest in Latin America.

Over the intervening years, intermarriage and, following the Revolution, mass emigration to the US has reduced the number of Chinese Cubans to around 400. Today, a movement to rediscover Barrio Chino's Chinese traditions is under way and the area around Calle Cuchillo and San Nicolás is distinguished by a Chinese gateway and a few Chinese restaurants. There is also a Chinese Cemetery on Calle 26 at the southwestern corner of the Cementerio de Colón (➤ this page).

🕂 185 D3 ⊠ Between Avenida Zanja and Calle Rayo, Centro

⓫ Parque John Lennon

El Jefe Maximo, Fidel Castro himself, unveiled the statue of John Lennon in this park, as a band played "All You Need is Love". The park had been known unofficially for years as Parque John Lennon, but the statue was installed only in 2000, because the music of The Beatles was actually banned for many years.

Life-size statue of John Lennon

In this quiet, shady park, a life-size bronze of the famous Beatle sits casually on a park bench. Inscribed on a plaque in front of him are the emotive words: *Dirás que soy un soñador, pero no soy el único* – "You may say I'm a dreamer, but I'm not the only one". It is a moving and optimistic tribute, and draws many visitors – so many that there is a 24-hour security guard, as John's glasses have been stolen twice.

🕂 184 A4 ⊠ Between Calle 15/17 and Calle 6/8, Vedado

⓬ Cementerio de Colón

Also known as the Necropolis Cristóbal Colón, the Spanish name for Christopher Columbus, this is Cuba's most important cemetery. It's a vast marble city of the dead. Entry is through a neoclassical gateway.

Cementerio de Colón holds the remains of Cuba's wealthiest and most powerful families

Established in 1871, the cemetery is in a grid design with a fine octagonal chapel (1886) at the heart. Many of the graves and mausoleums are elaborately executed in marble or granite, and some of Cuba's greatest leaders and richest families lie entombed here. Perhaps most celebrated of all is La Milagrosa, the tomb of Señora Amelia Goyri, who died in childbirth in 1901. It is believed that she was buried with the child beside her, but when disinterred for reburial the child was miraculously in her arms. Today, it's the heart of a popular cult and the tomb is covered with flowers.
➕ Off map 184 A3 ✉ Zapata and Calle 12, Vedado 🕐 Daily 8–5 💵 Inexpensive ❓ Guidebook with detailed map (CUC5) at ticket office. Guided tours free, but give a tip

🔢 **Plaza de la Revolución**
This large plaza in Nuevo Vedado is the focal point for Cuba's political rallies, notably the May Day Parade (1 May). It is dominated to the south by a huge granite statue of Cuban national hero José Martí (▶ 15). A star-shaped tower behind houses the **Museo José Martí**, backed by the government headquarters. On the north side of the plaza, the modernist Ministerio del Interior is fronted by a huge metal face of Che Guevara. In 2009, an equivalent visage of revolutionary leader Camilio Cienfuegos was added, with his famous words *"Vas bien, Fidel"* ("You're doing fine, Fidel").
➕ 184 A2

Museo José Martí
☎ (7) 859-2351 🕐 Mon–Sat 9–4:30 💵 Moderate

Lenin monument in Parque Lenin

14 Parque Lenin

This large park, 20km (12 miles) south of central Havana, is popular at weekends. An area of lakes, woods and parkland, with boating and horse-riding opportunities, it's home to a monument to Soviet revolutionary hero VI Lenin. In the vicinity, attractions include the vast Járdin Botánico Nacional, the Parque Zoológico Nacional and ExpoCuba, a huge exhibition displaying Cuba's achievements since 1959, all reached by taxi or your own transport.

Off map 184 C1   20km (12 miles) south of central Havana, Arroyo Naranjo   Tulipán   Inexpensive

15 Museo Hemingway

In 1939, American writer Ernest Hemingway (► 30–31) packed his bags and left Hotel Ambos Mundos (► 64), and bought a large house, Finca Vigía, 10km (6 miles) south of central Havana. Here he was to live until he left Cuba, just a year before his death in 1961. Today, the house is preserved as the Museo Hemingway, much as the writer left it, with thousands of books, numerous stuffed animals and the author's typewriter and Mannlicher carbine. In 2009, several thousand of Hemingway's digitalized, personal documents were made available to view. Visitors are not permitted to enter the building, but may only peer in through open windows and doors.

Off map 185 E1   15km (9.3 miles) southeast of central Havana, on Calle Vigía, San Francisco de Paula   Mon, Wed–Sat 9–4, Sun 9–12:30. Closed on rainy days   Moderate

16 Cojímar

This fishing village is famous for its association with Ernest Hemingway. It was here that he berthed his sport-fishing vessel, *Pilar*. The Hemingway Memorial featuring the author's bust stands by the seafront, near the old Spanish bastion Torreón de Cojímar (1649), and Hemingway's old bar, the Restaurante La Terraza (► 68), has been converted into a good seafood restaurant that is packed with Hemingway memorabilia.

179 E4   10km (6 miles) northeast of Havana on the road to the Playas del Este

Ernest Hemingway's desk in a quiet corner of Finca Vigía, now the Museo Hemingway

Where to...
Stay

Prices
Expect to pay per double room per night:
$ under CUC50 $$ CUC50–150 $$$ over CUC150

Ambos Mundos $$

Built in the 1920s, this modest but comfortable hotel is ideally located for Old Havana and is also a part of the Hemingway Trail (▶ 31). The great man lived here during the 1930s and his room – No 511 – is now preserved as a small museum, which you can visit even if you're not staying at the hotel. There's a piano bar offering live music nightly and an antique lift takes you to a rooftop bar. There are views across La Habana Vieja to the harbour.

🚩 185 F4 ☒ Calle Obispo 153, La Habana Vieja ☎ (7) 860-9530; www.habaguanexhotels.com

Casa de Jorge Coalla Potts $

Of Havana's many *casas particulares*, this is among the best for its location, cleanliness and splendid family environment. It's just three blocks from the Hotel Habana Libre, Coppelia and University of Havana. It has only one bedroom for rent but, if full, there are dozens of other *casas particulares* nearby.

🚩 184 A4 ☒ Calle 1456, between Calles 21 and 23 ☎ (7) 823-9032; www.havanaroomrental.com

Casa de Luis Batista $

In the very heart of Habana Vieja, this restored colonial home dates from 1717 and now operates as a *casa particular* run by the Batista family. It has lots of period detail, beginning with the nail-studded doors, a precious *alfarje* ceiling, and four guest rooms along a patio shaded by a red-tiled eave. Only two of the rooms can be legally rented, but you get to choose. Each is simply appointed but has air-conditioning, plus hot water in private bathrooms.

🚩 185 E4 ☒ Calle Amargura 255, between Calle Habana and Calle Compostela ☎ (7) 863-0622; www.havanacasaparticular.com

Florida $$$

A wonderful hotel, the Florida occupies a restored 18th-century mansion in the heart of Old Havana. There's a lot of period atmosphere both in the finely furnished rooms and in the colonial-style arches and pillars surrounding the cool central courtyard. The stylish restaurant offers quality *criollo* and international cuisine, and there's also a piano bar.

🚩 185 F4 ☒ Calles Obispo and Cuba, La Habana Vieja ☎ (7) 862-4127; www.habaguanexhotels.com

Nacional $$$

Havana's pre-eminent hotel (at least in size and prestige) since the 1930s, the Nacional dominates the central Malecón and the Vedado skyline from the bay. It's big and has two swimming pools, a business centre, tennis courts, barber's shop, pharmacy, banking (including advances on MasterCard and Visa), car rental and a guarded car park. Rooms are unexceptional, but there are attractive gardens. Famous people who have stayed here include Winston Churchill, Frank Sinatra and Ava Gardner. The location is central, the views superb and the menu fine but limited. The overall feel is a touch run-down.

🚩 184 A4 ☒ Calles 0 and 21, Vedado ☎ (7) 873-3564; www.hotelnacionaldecuba.com

Noemis y Wilfredo Havana $

This centrally located *casa particular*, just around the corner from Plaza Vieja, comes highly recommended. The lovely owners, Noemis and Wilfredo, could not be more friendly. The bedrooms, lounge and dining room are absolutely spotless, the breakfast costs just CUC4 and the laundry service is good value.

🕂 **185 F3** ⊠ **Calle Cuba 609, apartamento 2, between Santa Clara y Luz** ☎ **(7) 867 5229**

Raquel $$

A delightful historic hotel with art deco detailing throughout, the Raquel is superbly situated between Calle Obispo and Plaza Vieja. The lobby, supported by marble Corinthian columns, has an ornate mahogany bar and a lovely restaurant, and there's a solarium on the roof. Guest rooms have modern appliances and pleasing decor.

🕂 **185 F4** ⊠ **Calle San Ignacio and Amargura** ☎ **(7) 860-8280; www.hotelraquel-cuba.com**

Riviera $$

The Riviera is an old gangster's hotel, built by the "Jewish Godfather" Meyer Lansky (▶ 18–19) in 1957, just two years before Castro's revolution drove him to retirement in the nearby Bahamas. Some of the rooms have good views over the Straits of Florida. Unusually for Cuba, there are a few rooms which offer special facilities for visitors with a disability. The Riviera's general facilities and amenities include a lobby bar, restaurant, swimming pool, coffee shop by the pool, car rental and money exchange services. Because of the location in Vedado, you'll need to use a taxi to visit La Habana Vieja, but shops, restaurants and entertainment are nearby. A high point is the music at the Riviera's nightclub, the Palacio de Salsa. The buffet restaurant, though perfectly adequate, offers a limited choice.

🕂 **184 B4** ⊠ **Avenida Paseo and Malecón, Vedado** ☎ **(7) 836-4051; www.hotelhavanariviera.com**

Santa Isabel $$$

Originally the Palacio de los Condes de Santovenia, the building – dating from the early 19th century – became a hotel in 1867 when General Domingo Santovenia returned to Spain. The Santa Isabel was upgraded to five-star status, but it struggles to achieve this standard. Nevertheless, the hotel building exudes elegance, style and comfort. Located on the historic Plaza des Armas, the hotel's many rooms offer fine views across the heart of La Habana Vieja.

🕂 **185 F4** ⊠ **Calle Baratillo 9. Plaza de Armas, La Habana Vieja** ☎ **(7) 860-8201; www.hotelsantaisabel.com**

Saratoga $$$

Havana's premier hotel, the Saratoga is a deluxe option, which is under European management. It exudes a sophistication unrivalled throughout Cuba, with chic, contemporary decor and amenities to international standards. King-size beds – a rarity in Cuba – are standard in most rooms. Two bars and an exquisite Moorish-themed restaurant are among the highlights, but it also has a rooftop pool and gym. Its setting opposite El Capitolio is a bonus.

🕂 **185 E3** ⊠ **Paseo de Martí (Prado) 603, at Calle Dragones** ☎ **(7) 868-1000; www.hotel-saratoga.com**

Tryp Habana Libre $$$

This high-rise hotel in downtown Vedado dates from the 1950s. Apart from its superb location, the Habana Libre is also popular with visitors because of the wide range of services it offers. These include a second-floor swimming pool, the Turquino Cabaret on the 25th floor, a business centre (providing telephone and email) banking facilities, car rental services, a taxi stand and numerous shops, including a photography store and boutiques.

🕂 **184 A4** ⊠ **Calle L between Calles 23 and 25, Vedado** ☎ **(7) 834-6100; www.solmeliacuba.com/cuba-havana-hotels**

la Fondita Calle, Monserrate 557 Obispo

Where to...
Eat and Drink

Prices
Expect to pay per person for a two-course meal, excluding drinks and service:
$ under CUC10 $$ CUC10–25 $$$ over CUC25

Al Medina $$
Set in a beautifully restored colonial mansion, with charming breezy patio, this is one of Havana's top Middle Eastern restaurants, featuring Arab dishes based on lamb and couscous, mezze, hummus and falafel. The menu also features criollo (Cuban or Creole) specialities, though this is true more or less everywhere in Cuba. The Arab cuisine is primarily Lebanese, but the couscous indicates a Maghrebi influence.

🛨 185 F4 🗷 Calle Oficios 12, Calles Obispo and Obrapia, La Habana Vieja ☎ (7) 867-1041 🕒 Daily 12–12

Castillo de Farnes $$
An unassuming café on the corner of Monserrate conceals a small but elegant air-conditioned restaurant with friendly, English-speaking staff. Close to Parque Central, this is a little oasis with (by local standards) a fine selection of wines from Spain, France and Argentina, as well as Cuba. The ambience is enhanced by an art deco interior as well as by framed pictures of Fidel Castro, Raúl Castro and Ernesto "Che" Guevara eating and drinking here during the early days of the Revolution. The menu features criollo cuisine as well

as a selection of hors d'oeuvres. Specialities include Catalán-style chorizo con patatas en salsa (sausage and potatoes in a tomato and onion sauce), bacalao a la llauna (salted cod) and especially lobster boiled in its own juices. It's a great spot to spend a while people watching with a cocktail or coffee, and the waiters are delightful.

🛨 185 E4 🗷 Calles Monserrate and Obrapia, La Habana Vieja ☎ (7) 867-1030 🕒 Daily 12–12

Cocina de Lilliam $$
This paladar (private restaurant) is a winner with foreign diplomats and businessfolk – and no wonder. Set in a shaded garden, wrought-iron tables are arranged throughout a rambling brick patio, but there's also air-conditioned dining inside the 1930s house. Owner Lilliam Domínguez whips up some creative dishes. Her tartlets of tuna with onions and garbanzo (chickpea) appetizers are delicious, and for the main dish you can't go wrong

with her exquisite ropa vieja, a dish made of marinated and well-seasoned braised lamb. Reservations are essential.

🛨 Off map 184 A4 🗷 Calle 48 1311, between 13 and 15 ☎ (7) 209-6514 🕒 Mon–Sat 12–3, 7–11

El Aljibe $$
El Aljibe, an upmarket restaurant catering for the Cuban élite, business people, diplomats and affluent tourists, is enduringly popular and is certainly one of the best state-run restaurants serving Cuban criollo dishes. The house special is a delicious roast chicken in orange sauce, served with the most unusually tender Moros y Cristianos black beans and rice with plantains. Although it's a large restaurant, El Aljibe has an intimate atmosphere. Service is friendly, though when the restaurant is full it can be slow.

🛨 Off map 184 A5 🗷 71 Avenida 7, Calles 24 and 26, Miramar ☎ (7) 204-1583/4 🕒 Daily 12–12

La Bodeguita del Medio $$

This old Hemingway haunt displays black-and-white pictures of the author. A bohemian feel is cultivated, although the walls have been scrubbed clean of their old graffiti. The location near Plaza Vieja and the literary associations bring in many sightseers. To escape this constant flow, try the quieter, more comfortable roof terrace. Creole cuisine is the house speciality, and it's good. The *ajiaco* (pork and vegetable stew) with rice is recommended, but the troubadours who will hang around your table until they are tipped can be an irritation.

➕ 185 F4 ⊠ Calle Empedrado 207, between Calles San Ignacio and Cuba, La Habana Vieja ☎ (7) 863-1374 🕓 Daily 12–12

La Dominica $$

This predominantly Italian restaurant specializes in pasta dishes (usually variants of spaghetti) and pizza, but also offers a varied selection of Cuban *criollo* dishes – the beefsteak is unusually succulent and tender. It is renowned for its lobster, though it's not cheap. The efficient management is reflected both in the ambience and the better-than-average service. The location is excellent for strolling in La Habana Vieja, and it's a good place to sit and watch Cuban life go by over an iced beer.

➕ 185 F4 ⊠ Calle O'Reilly 108 and Mercaderes, La Habana Vieja ☎ (7) 860-2918 🕓 Daily 12–12

La Giraldilla $$$

A reliable, top end of the market restaurant, this has a Madrid-style tapas bar and attractive open-air terrace restaurant called El Patio los Naranjos (The Patio of Oranges). The wine list in the excellent basement Spanish restaurant, called La Bodega del Vino, is extensive, and includes European and New World vintages as well as local Cuban produce. It's attractively decorated with a timbered ceiling and antique-style ornaments and furniture and there's a live cabaret most evenings. Try the prawns steeped in garlic and flame-grilled lobster served with a Ricard sauce.

➕ Off map 184 A4 ⊠ Calles 222 and 37, La Lisa ☎ (7) 273-0568 🕓 Daily 10am–midnight

La Guarida $$$

Havana's most remarkable restaurant, this one is a joint operation — a *paladar* actually sponsored by the Ministry of Culture. On the third floor of a virtually derelict building, it's reached via a much-decayed winding marble staircase, popular for fashion shoots (including a famous Playboy nude portfolio). Prior to opening as a restaurant, the former private residence was a setting in the hit movie *Fresa y Chocolate*. Decorated in the style of a Parisian bistro, the walls are festooned with original artwork, aged prints and photos of international celebrities who've dined here. The owners once lived in France and the menu shows it, combining Cuban ingredients with French dishes to come up with combinations such as *tartar de atún* (tuna) and chicken breast with pepper sauce. Some dishes disappoint, but the entire experience makes this restaurant one of the best dining options in Cuba. The place is always packed, and reservations are advised. Be aware that La Guarida is in a rough, run-down area where muggings are known, so it's best to take a taxi.

➕ 184 C4 ⊠ Calle Concordia 418 between Gervasio and Escobar ☎ (7) 862-4940; www.laguarida.com 🕓 Daily 12–4, 7–12

La Paella $$

La Paella's proud boast is that it offers the best and most authentic Castilian paella in Cuba. Other popular dishes on the menu include barbecued shrimp and lobster. The atmosphere is authentically Spanish – very Costa Brava, with traditional Iberian decor and wooden screens.

The service is good, the wine list fairly extensive (though the wines are predominantly Spanish and Cuban). The prices are quite high but not unreasonable.

🗺 185 F4 ⊠ Calles Oficios and Obrapía, La Habana Vieja ☎ (7) 671037 ⊙ Daily 12–11

La Terraza $$

One of Hemingway's preferred haunts, this is an unpretentious but clean and welcoming seaside restaurant overlooking Cojímar's old Spanish fort. Fronted by a bar-café, the restaurant has 15 red-clothed tables in an airy room featuring numerous framed pictures of "Papa Hemingway". Prices are perhaps a bit high, but you're paying for a little piece of history as well as your meal. The menu is unusually extensive for contemporary Cuba and features seafood. The house speciality – lobsters – are kept live in a tank near a bust of the great man. Other dishes include various combinations of pork, chicken, shrimp, oysters, tuna and ham.

There's a good selection of wines featuring Château de Rochefort, Rosé de Loire and Pouilly Fumé. The "Gregorio Fuentes" cocktail is worth trying.

🗺 179 E4 ⊠ Calle Real 161 and Calle Candelaria, Cojímar, Habana Este ☎ (7) 939232 ⊙ Daily 12–11

Los Nardos $–$$

This very reasonably priced place opposite El Capitolio is probably the best restaurant in the city, but there are actually three different restaurants in this building – be sure to eat at Los Nardos. It is justifiably extremely popular so be prepared to queue as reservations are not accepted; you are advised to arrive early to secure a table. The ramshackle exterior of the building belies a jewel of an interior featuring high ceilings and decorated in traditional Cuban style with mahogany furniture, where you can dine on lobster, rich fish soup and classic Cuban dishes to the sounds of the resident pianist.

Portions are enormous, so consider sharing dishes.

🗺 185 E3 ⊠ Paseo de Martí 563 ☎ (7) 863-2985 ⊙ Daily 12–11

Restaurante Hanoi $

Restaurante Hanoi dates from the days when Cuba and North Vietnam were both considered to be close ideological allies of the Soviet Union. This friendly and inexpensive establishment offers an unusual but pleasing *criollo* version of standard Vietnamese cuisine at budget prices.

🗺 185 E3 ⊠ Calles Brasil and Bernaza, La Habana Vieja ☎ (7) 867-1029 ⊙ Daily 12–11

Santo Ángel $$

Set in an attractive restored colonial building, formerly the Colegio El St Angelo founded in 1866, this restaurant overlooks Old Havana's Plaza Vieja. You can eat inside or on the colonnaded terrace outside. Dishes include *pollo a la Cubana* (Creole-style chicken), as well

as *especialidades de la casa tablas* (house specialties) such as *pescado* (fish), *mariscos* (seafood) and *embutidos* (sausage) platters. Most noteworthy is the delicious *muelitas de cangrejo con miel y ajo* (crab claws with honey and garlic). Troubadors provide entertainment.

🗺 185 F3 ⊠ Plaza Vieja and Calle San Ignacio, La Habana Vieja ☎ (7) 861-1626 ⊙ Daily 11–11

Taberna de la Muralla $$

An excellent tavern, this place has its own microbrewery producing satisfyingly cold draught beer. Well-positioned in the southwest corner of Plaza Vieja, with delightful views, it sells beer by the glass or the jug together with a selection of tasty dishes. These range from snacks, such as hamburgers and pizzas, to *bistec de cerdo con papas fritas* (pork steak and fries). Cooling fans stir the air.

🗺 185 F3 ⊠ Calles San Ignacio and Muralla, Plaza Vieja, La Habana Vieja ☎ (7) 866-4453 ⊙ Daily 11am–1pm

Where to... Shop

Until recently, Socialist Cuba had set its face firmly against both consumerism and private property ownership. The extremely rapid development of international tourism in the first decade of the 21st century means that this situation is changing – especially in Havana. The back streets and narrow alleys of La Habana Vieja are a strange mix of poorly stocked government peso shops and new, stylish, luxury stores offering imported goods and better-quality local produce for non-negotiable convertible peso prices. The best streets to explore for shopping include Calle Obispo, Calle O'Reilly and Calle Obrapía. There are also more upmarket shopping opportunities available in Vedado and Miramar.

SOUVENIRS

Hard-currency shops within hotels and all-inclusive resorts sell items such as dolls, woodcarvings, jewellery, stamps and coins. There's sometimes a good selection of books, but almost all of them are about the Cuban revolution and especially Che Guevara and Fidel. T-shirts and Che-style berets are ubiquitous and enduringly popular. In Vedado, try the Habana Libre (▶ 65), in Centro go to the Nacional (▶ 64) and, in Miramar, the Sierra Maestra at Avenida 1, between Calles 0 and 2. In La Habana Vieja, Calle Obispo and Mercaderes offer plenty of opportunities for souvenir shopping, as does the artisans' market on Avenida Desamparados.

LOCAL PRODUCE

Two of Cuba's finest local products are rum and cigars (▶ 9–11). These are among the best in the world. Avoid buying these products from private traders on the street, as most of the cigars are fake and may be confiscated at the airport on your departure. In Havana, cigars and rum are widely available at all government hotels, but don't miss the opportunity to visit the Fábrica de Tabacos Partagás (▶ 60–61), which sells the best cigars at the end of each tour. Also worthy of note is the excellent local Cuban coffee. Cubita, Turquina and Hola are the top brands and are available at most branches of the hard-currency chain Tiendas Panamericanas, or at the airport.

MUSIC

All manner of Cuban music is available on CD throughout Havana. Performers at nightclubs and even on street corners will approach you with copies of their own music, but once again it's probably best to buy through government outlets. The Cuban State Recording Company, Egrem (www.egrem.com.cu), produces high-quality CDs, and you can be sure you are getting the real thing. Its main outlet is Casa de la Música Egrem, at Galiano y Neptuno. Musical instruments are also popular souvenirs, from maracas through guitars to violins. For all things musical, visit Artex on Calles 23 and L (opposite the Habana Libre Hotel). Also good is the Palacio de la Artesanía, at Calle Cuba 64, in La Habana Vieja.

ART

Numerous art galleries and street markets in Havana sell paintings, prints and sculptures by local Cuban artists. There's quite a range of styles on show, from Socialist Realism through Cuban-style

Impressionism to Modern Art. Be sure to buy at an approved state outlet and keep the receipt, or your artwork may be confiscated by the airport customs. All the squares of La Habana Vieja (▶ 54–56) have **art markets**, though the best are to be found at the Plaza de la Catedral (Tue–Sun; ▶ 59–60) and in the eastern part of the Old City by the Castillo de la Real Fuerza. There are also art markets at the citadels of El Morro and La Cabaña (▶ 57–58). More expensive paintings, by artists of international renown, are found in **art shops** along Calle Obispo.

ANTIQUES AND SECOND-HAND BOOKS

There isn't much of a trade in antiques, as the Cuban authorities are intent on preserving antiquities, and their interpretation of what is a "national treasure" can be random and severe. Second-hand books are another matter – Cuba is a society which places a high value on literacy, and book markets can provide some real bargains. The **Plaza de Armas** (▶ 54) in Old Havana is the best and liveliest second-hand book market (closed on Mondays). Most books are in Spanish and are mostly pre-revolutionary texts, but writings in English, French, German and even Russian are also available. There are no fixed prices or government controls – bargain hard. Also on Plaza de Armas try **Librería Bella Habana**, at the Palacio del Segundo Cabo. Another bookstore worth browsing is **La Moderna Poesía**, at Calle Obispo near Parque Central. Opposite La Moderna Poesía is **La Internacional**, selling titles for pesos and convertible pesos.

IMPORTED GOODS

Scarce imported goods, such as speciality foods, brand-name clothing, toiletries, electronic items and cameras, are sometimes available at special government stores and can be purchased only with convertibles pesos. In La Habana Vieja, the best of these is **Harris Brothers** behind the Edificio Bacardí on Calle Zulueta (near the Plaza Hotel), but despite the store's hard-currency status, and goods being spread out over four floors, supplies remain limited. Beyond La Habana Vieja, the main shopping streets of Centro are **Calles Neptuno**, **San Miguel** and **San Rafael** – not that there's always much for sale on the shelves. In Vedado, most luxury hotels have boutiques selling quality imported fashions and jewellery. In Miramar (the relatively affluent embassy district), the large **5 y 42 Complex**, at Calle 42 and Avenida 5 has stores selling imported luxuries for hard-currency shoppers, including a wide selection of speciality food items. Also in Miramar at Avenida 3 and Calle 70, the well-stocked **Diplotienda**, once exclusively for foreign diplomats, is now open to anyone with hard currency.

HARD-CURRENCY FOOD CHAINS

A new phenomenon proving popular with Cubans who have access to convertible pesos, and invaluable to foreign visitors needing to stock up on everyday items, is the government-owned chain **Tiendas Panamericanas**. Imported foodstuffs, cosmetics, toiletries and drinks are available here, though there's no guarantee that shelves, once depleted, will be restocked for weeks at a time. Branches of Tiendas Panamericanas can be found both in Havana and at larger destinations across the country. This is the best and most reliable place to go to buy bottled water (both still and sparkling), instant coffee, imported sauces to spice up the often rather bland *criollo* cuisine, shampoo, toothpaste and many other everyday necessities that are frequently unavailable elsewhere in Cuba. Only convertible pesos are accepted at Tiendas Panamericanas.

Where to...
Be Entertained

Under socialism, Havana might appear to be but a shadow of its former vibrant self, yet Habaneros are inventive and insist on having a good time. It's true that the seedier side of pre-revolutionary Havana has been severely circumscribed, but many people would consider this a good thing. It's also true that, under Castro, the arts have been encouraged, with classical music, ballet and drama thriving. Yet some sections of the population, notably gays, have suffered severe persecution, while Carnival (► 44) – for years discouraged as frivolous – is making a comeback. Fortunately, as a result of the tourism boom, Havana is coming alive again, although some of the best venues are off-limits to Cuban members of the public.

THE ARTS

Top of the list must be La Habana Vieja's **Gran Teatro**, at Paseo de Martí 458 (► 60). Regular performances of classical music and ballet are held, and prices are generally low. A dress code is enforced. Classical music and jazz can be seen at **Teatro Amadeo Roldán**, at Avenida 7 and Calle D in Vedado. For avant-garde dance and theatre, try **Teatro Mella**, at Calles 7 and A, also in Vedado. The **Teatro Nacional de Cuba**, by the Plaza de la Revolución at Paseo and Calle 39, puts on classical and contemporary music, drama and dance. The **Conjunto Folklórico Nacional de Cuba**, at 103 Calle 4, Calzada in Vedado, has top Afro-Cuban music and dance.

MUSIC AND DANCE

Informal and spontaneous musical events characterize Habanero life. **Cumbanchas** (street parties) and **pesas** (jam sessions) can occur anywhere at almost any time. Information is passed on by word of mouth, but if you're not part of the grapevine, just follow the sounds of son, samba, chá-chá-chá and rumba – you'll be made most welcome. **Club Salseando Chevere**, at Márgenes del Río Almendares, Calle 49 and Avenida 28 in Miramar (www.club-salseando-chevere.com; Wed 6–11), is a popular weekly salsa party, with a bit of mumba and rumba. It attracts a lot of tourists, but is good fun and includes a performance by professionals. The two venues of **Casa de la Música**, at Avenida 20, esq 35, Miramar and Calle Galianao 225 are both great spots for rum drinking (buy a bottle), live music and dancing. **Jazz Café**, on the third floor of the shopping mall Galerías de Paseo,

at Avenida Paseo and Avenida 3, in Vedado, hosts some excellent jazz musicians. In Vedado, **El Gran Palenque**, at 103 Calle 4, Calzada is an Afro-Cuban rumba venue run by the Conjuncto Folklórico Nacional de Cuba (Sat 3–5).

NIGHTLIFE

Havana's nightlife is justifiably legendary. There's a wealth of discos, bars, nightclubs and downmarket holes-in-the-wall. At the top end, only hard-currency holders are able to gain access, but local discos and bars are open to all and sundry. The most popular venues are constantly changing, so it makes sense to ask around – your hotel reception desk will have a good idea of what's happening and when. The website wwwcubaabsolutelycom has a monthly What's On guide for Havana that is full of information about everything from the arts and dance to the latest karaoke and rap venues, and is regularly updated.

Otherwise, as elsewhere in Havana, follow the beat. Top, although touristy, bars include **La Bodeguita del Medio** (▶ 67), at Calle Empedrado 207 and **El Floridita**, at Calle Obispo 557, both formerly haunts of Ernest Hemingway and both in La Habana Vieja. Over in Vedado, **Salón Turquino**, at the Tryp Habana Libre hotel (▶ 65), with its nightly cabaret/disco and spectacular rooftop that rolls back to reveal the starry night sky, is enduringly popular, as is the **Jazz Café**, at Galerías de Paseo, Calles Paseo and 1 in Vedado – featuring live jazz nightly. Another tremendous venue for jazz is the basement **La Zorra y el Cuervo**, at La Rampa between Calle M and Calle O. It gets packed and is smoky, but many of the country's up-and-coming jazz artists play alongside well-known greats.

Just about every hotel has a bar. For bolero you might check out **Café Concierto Gato Tuerto**, at Calle O, 17/19 in Vedado. If you want to walk on the dark side, try the area between Parque Central and Avenida Italia – there are small, seedy but authentically atmospheric bars in this area. Take sensible precautions with your valuables.

DISCOS

Macumba Habana, at La Giraldilla, Calle 222, 37/51, is an open-air disco often preceded by fashion shows or cabaret. For salsa, try the **Cabaret Copa Room**, at Hotel Riviera at Paseo and Malecón. **Patio de Maria**, at Calle 37 between Paseo and Calle 2, offers a Cuban mix of rock music and salsa. There's a disco-cabaret at the **Habana Café**.

CABARET

The casinos and sex shows of pre-revolutionary Havana are long gone, together with the gangsters who ran them (▶ 18–19). Now Las Vegas-style floorshows rule the roost, mostly featuring scantily clad dancers with tiny g-strings, elaborate head-dresses, feather boas and the like. The most extravagant and opulent of these is the **Cabaret Tropicana**, at 4504 Calle 72, Mariano, in the far west of the city (closed Mondays). If you don't want to go so far out of town, a good alternative is the **Cabaret Parisién**, at the Hotel Nacional (▶ 64). It's best to reserve in advance for these shows, especially if you're planning on visiting the Tropicana. Entry prices usually include a drink. The shows are sexy, but not decadent.

CINEMA

There are more than 150 cinemas in Havana, but most are very run-down. Films are shown in their original language and subtitled if the original is in English. There are generally two shows a day, at 5pm and 8pm. The best is **Cine Payret**, at Paseo de Marti 505, opposite the Capitolio. Dating from 1878, this luxurious cinema has five or six screenings a day. In Vedado, go to **Cine Yara**, at the intersection of Calles 23 and L, which opens at noon and has screenings throughout the day.

FESTIVALS

The big event in Havana was once the **Carnaval de La Habana**, celebrated every July along Paseo de Marti and Malecón. For a couple of decades, it was considered frivolous and counter-revolutionary, but now it's back. Featuring processions, floats, music and dance, it is much more amateurish than the equivalent event in Santiago de Cuba (▶ 137). Other important Havana festivals (▶ 44) include the **International Jazz Festival** in late November, the **International Guitar Festival** (biennial) in May, the **International Ballet Festival** (biennial) at the Gran Teatro and other venues in October/November, and the **New Latin American Film Festival**, in early December.

Western Cuba

Getting Your Bearings

Although closer to Havana than almost any other part of the country, western Cuba is relatively isolated and relaxed in atmosphere. It also differs from the central and eastern plains in that tobacco is the most important crop, not sugar.

The main link between Havana and Pinar del Río, the chief city of the west, is the *autopista* (motorway). It's not a long or particularly arduous journey, but within a couple of hours you'll find you have left sophisticated Havana for a town of horse-drawn carriages and moustachioed, cigar-smoking *guajiros* (country people). Beyond Pinar, with its faded colonial architecture, the west has much to offer.

Archipiélago de los Colorados
Bahía de la Mulata
Puerto Esperanza
Pan de
La
Santa Lucía
Palma
Viñales
Minas de Matahambre
Consolación del Sur
Cabeza
PINAR DEL RÍO
Arroyos de Mantua
San Juan y Martínez
Pinar del Río
Mantua
San Luis
La Colom
Vuelta Abajo 4
Golfo de La Manigua
Guanahacabibes
Isabel Rubio
Bahía de Cartas
Punta la Fija
Parque Nacional de Península de Guanahacabibes
Bahía de Guadiana
La Fé
Punta
Cortes
Manuel Lazo
Parque Naciona San Felipe
Punta Cajón
Península de Guanahacabibes
Valle San Juan
Cabo Francés
Cayo Real
Cayo Co
Las Tumbas
Bahía de Corrientes
María la Gorda
Cabo de San Antonio
Cabo Corrientes
Cayos L
Parq Pur Punta
Punta

★ Don't Miss

At Your Leisure

Previous page: A magnificent beach at Cayo Largo

Left: Sierra del Rosario, a popular weekend retreat

To the north, the lush hills of the Sierra del Rosario shelter a wide diversity of wildlife, as well as two very appealing hill resorts – Soroa and Las Terrazas. A minor road, the *Circuito Norte* (➤ 154–155), leads back to Havana via the attractive shores of the Gulf of Mexico, giving fine views over the Archipiélago de Colorados.

Immediately north of Pinar del Río, the old village and valley of Viñales (➤ 153–154) have an enduring appeal that regularly draws many visitors. To the west, minor roads lead to San Juan y Martínez and the tobacco hub of Vuelta Abajo, before winding still farther westwards to the dive centre of Punta María La Gorda.

In Four Days

If you're not quite sure where to begin your travels, this itinerary recommends four practical and enjoyable days out in western Cuba, taking in some of the best places to see using the Getting Your Bearings map on the previous page. For more information, see the main entries.

Day 1

Morning
Drive to **❶ Pinar del Río** (➤ 78–80), the laid-back cultural and commercial capital of far-western Cuba.

Afternoon
After briefly exploring the town on foot, drive to **❹ Vuelta Abajo** (below; ➤ 87), the best-known cigar tobacco-producing district in Cuba and indeed the world. Visit Finca Pinar San Luís – the world-famous tobacco farm – before returning to **❶ Pinar del Río**.

Evening
Sample a *Guayabita del Pinar* (➤ 78) at one of the bars on **Calle Martí**, before heading to the **Cabaret Rumayor** (➤ 93) for a vibrant cabaret show.

Day 2

Morning
Drive north from **❶ Pinar del Río** (➤ 78–80) through the lovely valley of **Viñales** (➤ 154). Spend the morning exploring the village and valley.

Afternoon
Take the picturesque but pot-holed **Circuito Norte** (➤ 154) to the mountain resort of **5 Soroa** (➤ 87), a popular weekend retreat, where it is possible to have dinner in the hotel restaurant.

Evening
Return to Havana and get a good night's sleep, in preparation for an early flight in the morning.

Day 3

Morning
Take a taxi to Havana Airport and fly to the **2 Archipiélago de los Canarreos** – you can choose between **Nueva Gerona** (➤ 82) or **Cayo Largo** (right; ➤ 83).

Afternoon
Either explore the unique environment of the **Isla de la Juventud** (➤ 81), or enjoy some of the best swimming and diving anywhere in the world at **Cayo Largo.**

Evening
Consider having dinner at El Dragón (➤ 83) before flying back to Havana for the night.

Day 4

Morning
Choose from busy **6 Varadero** (➤ 88) or the more isolated **10 Playa Girón** (➤ 90). To get to Varadero, drive east along the northern coast road to **3 Matanzas** (➤ 84–86). For Playa Girón, head south along the *autopista nacional* to the **8 Península de Zapata** (➤ 89).

Afternoon
Either explore the sleepy town of **7 Cárdenas** (➤ 88–89), with its horse-drawn buses and famous cathedral and Columbus statue, before heading into Varadero; or visit the historic **9 Bahía de Cochinos** (➤ 89) before continuing to **10 Playa Girón** (➤ 90).

Evening
Check into one of the upmarket hotels in **6 Varadero** (➤ 88) or a beach resort at Playa Girón.

❶ Pinar del Río

Pinar del Río is one of Cuba's largest provinces, taking up much of the western part of the island. Despite it's relative proximity to Havana, it has traditionally been viewed as a rural, even unsophisticated, area. The *autopista* connecting Pinar del Río town with Havana, built by the communist authorities more than 20 years ago, was meant to change all this – but there's little traffic, and Pinar remains a remarkably quiet and laid-back destination.

Pinar del Río is – or rather was – Cuba's "cigar city". The surrounding fertile land is ideally suited to producing tobacco, and during the 19th century the entire region grew relatively prosperous on the strength of this one crop. This wealth explains the many elegant, if faded, haciendas and townhouses that still dot the region. There is plenty of evidence that Pinar was once a fairly rich town.

No more. In the late 19th century, the major cigar-producing factories moved their operations to nearby Havana, and Pinar del Río lost much of its wealth, becoming an agricultural backwater. Unfortunately, six decades of communist neglect has resulted in the fine old colonial buildings falling into serious disrepair – but most are not beyond restoration, and in time, as tourism flourishes, Pinar should once again become a small city of quiet elegance.

Palacio Guasch
Pinar's important sights include the **Museo de Ciencias Naturales** (Museum of Natural Science), also known locally as the Palacio Guasch, which houses a collection of stuffed animals, birds and preserved insects from all over the world. It was established by a local doctor, Francisco Guasch, in 1914. A world traveller, he brought back not just preserved insects and wildlife of all kinds, but also an unusual and eclectic taste for various styles of architecture, ranging from Gothic, through Moorish to Roman. These are combined in the stucco towers and frontage of the Palacio Guasch, which also houses a collection of concrete dinosaurs in its back garden. The eccentric architecture makes the museum hard to miss.

Rum and Cigar Factories
About 200m (220 yards) south from the town centre intersection of Calle Martí and Isabel Rubio stands a small factory, the **Fábrica de Bebidas Guayabita**. This is the only distillery in the world producing *Guayabita del Pinar* liquor, often billed as a brandy but in fact a fortified and specially flavoured rum. Distilled rum is brought to the factory and sealed in oak casks together with locally grown pink *guayabita* or baby guava. It's 40 per cent proof and sells for around CUC5 a bottle – a bargain that is uniquely Pinarese.

El Aljiba Restaurant.

The interior of Catedral de San Rosendo

Hotel Vuelta Abajo in Calle Martí, the main street of Pinar del Río

Guided tours of the factory include a liquor tasting as well as the almost obligatory Cuban attempt to sell you some cigars. Tours are given in Spanish and in English.

Just a couple of hundred metres northwest of the **Catedral de San Rosendo** – Pinar's finest church, built in 1883, and chiefly notable for its stained-glass windows – is the **Fábrica de Tabacos Francisco Donatién**, the town's small yet famous cigar factory. As with the Fábrica de Bebidas Guayabita, the management are only too pleased to welcome visitors and show them around. Here you can see workers hand-rolling the cigars (be prepared for a smoky atmosphere – employees are free to smoke as many as they wish) and follow the various processes of cigar production from dried leaf to finished product. The factory shop will do its best to sell you cigars – the premium brand is Vegueros – while the poorly paid workers are not above begging as you pass by.

If you are interested in 19th-century Pinar del Río, visit the
Museo Provincial de Historia. This is housed in a colonial
mansion and filled with moribund memorabilia, including a
dining room of the era, with a painting of tobacco fields.

Hand-rolling tobacco at the cigar factory

TAKING A BREAK
Try the restaurant in the Hotel Vuelta Abajo (➤ 91).
Inexpensive pizzas are available at stores along Calle Martí.

✚ 178 C3

Museo de Ciencias Naturales
✉ Calle Martí Este 202 ☎ (48) 753087 🕓 Mon–Sat 9–4:45, Sun 9–12:45
💷 Inexpensive

Fábrica de Bebidas Guayabita
✉ Calle Isabel Rubio Sur 189 ☎ (48) 752966 🕓 Mon–Fri 9–4, Sat 9–1
💷 Inexpensive

Fábrica de Tabacos Francisco Donatién
✉ Calle Antonio Maceo Oeste 157 ☎ (48) 753069 🕓 Mon–Fri 9–12, 1–4,
Sat–Sun 9–12 💷 Moderate

Museo Provincial de Historia
✉ Calle Martí Este 58 ☎ (48) 754300 🕓 Mon 12–4, Tue–Sat 9–8
💷 Inexpensive

PINAR DEL RÍO: INSIDE INFO

Top tip Take a **horse-and-carriage** tour for an authentic feel of this antiquated
and isolated town.

One to miss Watch out for hustlers who will try to sell you **illegal (unlicensed)**
cigars, which will be confiscated at Havana Airport.

2 Archipiélago de los Canarreos

Although strictly speaking the chain of islands that makes up the Archipiélago de los Canarreos is part of Western Cuba, it's geographically quite different. Separated from the mainland by the 100km-wide (60-mile) Golfo de Batabanó, it is only accessible by air from Havana or by ferry from Surgidero de Batabanó, in Havana Province.

The archipelago itself is not well served with communications. If you wish to travel from the larger Isla de la Juventud in the west to the popular beach resorts of Cayo Largo del Sur in the east, you will have to return to Havana to board a new flight back out again (book as far ahead as possible, as the flights from Havana are very popular). The high-speed catamaran-ferry service from Surgidero de Batabanó may be relatively cheap, but it's also quite unreliable.

The jetty at Punta Frances beach on Isla de la Juventud

The main island in the archipelago, long known as the "Island of Pines" and now as the **Isla de la Juventud**, is where most Cubans live and fewest tourists stay. Known colloquially as "La Isla", its isolation means it has long been used for a variety of criminal activities, and was once also known to British privateers as "Parrot Island", a hiding place from official authorities.

Later it became infamous as the site of the **Presidio Modelo**, a harsh isolation prison for political detainees and dangerous criminals. Fidel Castro was held here for some months after his attack on the Moncada Barracks in 1953. The Presidio Modelo is the island's most interesting site. However, as an alternative to the prison towers (although long since disused), most visitors choose to visit the spectacular **dive sites** of the hundreds of cays and islands with their coral canyons and hulking historical shipwrecks.

The Main Town

The capital of Isla de la Juventud, **Nueva Gerona**, is a
pleasant place. Founded in 1830, its chief exports are citrus
fruits and marble. The main church, **Iglesia Nuestra Señora
de los Dolores**, overlooks **Parque Julio Antonio Mella**, the
town's central square. It's a somnolent place, without a great
deal to see apart from the **Museo de la Lucha Clandestina**
(Museum of the Clandestine Struggle). Southwest of town,
you will find the **Museo Finca El Abra**, a farmhouse-turned-
museum where José Martí, the great Cuban patriot, was held
under house arrest for three months in the late 19th century.

It's not the bucolic charm of Nueva Gerona that draws
foreign visitors to "La Isla", but the numerous dive sites off
the **Costa de los Piratas** (Pirate Coast). This area, reputedly
filled with the wrecks of sunken Spanish galleons and
English and Dutch pirate vessels, lies south of the large bay
known as **Bahía de Siguanea** off the west coast of the island.
A number of Spanish and other wrecks are preserved in
reasonable condition in the warm waters of the bay, teeming
with fish and easily accessible to trained divers. Here, too, is
the **Caribbean Cathedral**, supposedly the tallest living coral
column in the world.

Cayo Largo
is famed for
its soft, white
beaches and
turquoise
waters

Isolated Islands

Cayo Largo is the largest of the small group
of cays which make up the eastern half of the
Archipiélago de los Canarreos. Just 24km
(15 miles) long and shaped like a sickle moon,
Cayo Largo is 200km (124 miles) southeast
of Havana and more than 100km (60 miles)
east of the Isla de la Juventud. It's dedicated to
international tourism – most of the Cubans here
are working in the service industry.

Cayo Largo is indeed spectacular – the sugar-
white beaches and turquoise waters are gorgeous.
If you're looking for a Robinson Crusoe paradise
Cayo Largo is probably the place. The only
activities are wining, dining, sunbathing and –
above all – swimming, snorkelling and diving.
There's even a nudist beach at Playa Blanca (most
unusual for Cuba, where topless bathing is not
culturally acceptable). It's also possible to charter
private boats for trips to other, nearby deserted
cays – and scuba-diving courses are available.
This is a great place for a complete break away
from it all, but there's almost nothing genuinely
Cuban about Cayo Largo.

TAKING A BREAK

For quasi-Chinese cuisine, try a meal at
Restaurante El Dragón (➤ 93), at Calle 39 in
Nueva Gerona.

✚ 179 D3

Presidio Modelo
✉ 4km (2.5 miles) east of Nueva Gerona at Reparto Chacón
☎ (46) 325112 🕐 Mon–Sat 8–4, Sun 8–12 💷 Inexpensive

Museo de la Lucha Clandestina
✉ Calles 24 and 45 ☎ (46) 324582 🕐 Tue–Sat 9–5, Sun 8–12
💷 Inexpensive

Museo Finca El Abra
✉ 3km (1.8 miles) southwest of Nueva Gerona 🕐 Tue–Sat 9–4, Sun 9–1
💷 Inexpensive

ARCHIPIÉLAGO DE LOS CANARREOS: INSIDE INFO

Top tips **Don't try to bring cigars** from Nueva Gerona to the mainland unless you
have an authentic certificate of government sale. The customs authorities
between the archipelago and the mainland are thorough.

■ If you're in Nueva Gerona anytime between October and March, try to catch
a baseball game at the **Estadio Cristóbal Labra**.

■ A great way to explore Nueva Gerona and around is by horse cart or
carretone. These are available for rent from the main square for reasonable
rates, but you may want to negotiate for hourly, or even daily fares.

3 **Matanzas**

Matanzas is sometimes referred to as the "Athens of Cuba" because of its rich cultural and literary traditions. It was once a major exporter of livestock to Spain and remains a relatively prosperous port city, with a number of impressive churches and civic buildings.

The coast road east from Havana runs past a series of attractive beaches known as the **Playas del Este** before entering Matanzas Province at the remarkable **Mirador de Bacunayagua**, a raised viewpoint overlooking Cuba's highest (110m/360ft) and longest (314m/1,030ft) bridge, spanning a deep ravine, which separates the two provinces. There's a restaurant here, on a small hill to the left (north) of the road. It's worth stopping to have a cool drink and gaze down into the ravine, which is lined with royal palms and is usually filled with wheeling turkey buzzards sailing on the wind.

An Ancient Entrepot

Matanzas is a medium-sized port city with a population of around 140,000. It grew wealthy in the 17th and 18th centuries as an importer of slaves and an exporter of livestock. Its real heyday came in the 19th century, however, when sugar and coffee began to be exported in bulk from the sheltered Bahía de Matanzas. In 1843 the railway from Havana reached the town, and Matanzas became, for a brief period, Cuba's second city.

The historic heart of Old Matanzas dates from this time, and it is here that most of the worthwhile sights are found. It's not a large area, located between the Río Yumurí to the north and the Río San Juan to the south, and can be explored comfortably on foot in about an hour.

Historic Heart

The heart of Matanzas is **Plaza de la Vigía**, and this is a good place to start an exploration of the city. In the middle of the square is a statue dedicated to the Cuban independence hero Antonio Maceo, while just across from this the neoclassical **Parque de los Bomberos**, built in 1897, still houses the city's fire brigade. On the opposite side of the square is the **Galería de Arte Provincial** (Provincial Art Gallery), while facing the art gallery is the neoclassical **Teatro Sauto** (1862), with marble statues of Greek goddesses standing in the entrance hall. However, it's the feel of the Plaza de la Vigía rather than any of the particular buildings that give this part of central Matanzas its special atmosphere.

Next door to the Provincial Art Gallery is the **Ediciones Vigía**, a real craftsman's factory producing hand-bound, limited-edition books. You can watch them being made – they are real works of art – and perhaps purchase a copy as a special souvenir.

Monument to José Martí in Parque Libertad

The Ecclesiastical Core

To the west, behind Plaza de la Vigía, a series of narrow streets lined with some attractive colonnaded buildings leads for several hundred metres into the heart of the old city. Here, you will find the **Catedral de San Carlos Borromeo**, one of the city's finest buildings. Originally constructed in 1693, it was restored in the mid-19th century. Unfortunately, it is in serious need of further renovation. Close by is **Parque Libertad**, with a statue to the national hero José Martí.

The south side of Parque Libertad is home to another of Matanzas' unusual institutions, the **Museo Farmacéutico**, which dates from the 1880s. This fine traditional pharmacy has been preserved as a museum, complete with its original ceramic and glass medicine jars, strongly built hardwood cabinets and medicinal prescriptions.

Away from the heart of town, in the more northerly district of Versalles, the old **Castillo San Severino** has been partly restored and today hosts the interesting **Museo de la Ruta del Esclavo** (Slave Route Museum), including a section devoted to Cuba's African-derived religions.

TAKING A BREAK

There are a few cheap local restaurants serving sandwiches, but the best place in town is the **Café Atenas** (tel: (45) 253493, daily 10–10) on Plaza de la Vigía, which serves spaghetti and pizza, and a tasty shrimp enchilada.

A 19th-century chemist's shop is preserved as Museo Farmacéutico

🕂 179 F4

Galería de Arte Provincial
✉ Calle 272, Plaza de la Vigía ⏱ Mon–Fri 9–5, Sat 1–5 👆 Free

Ediciones Vigía
✉ Calle 272, Plaza de la Vigía ☎ (45) 244845 ⏱ Mon–Fri 9–6
👆 Inexpensive

Catedral de San Carlos Borromeo
✉ Calle 282 ⏱ Mon–Fri 8–12, Sat–Sun 9–12 👆 Free, donations welcome

Museo Farmacéutico
✉ Calle 83 Milanés 4951 ☎ (45) 243179 ⏱ Daily 10–5 👆 Inexpensive

Museo de la Ruta del Esclavo
✉ Calle 57 ☎ (45) 283259 ⏱ Tue–Sat 9–4, Sun 9–12 👆 Inexpensive

MATANZAS: INSIDE INFO

Top tips Visit Matanzas as a **day trip** from either Havana or Varadero, or better still en route from Havana to Varadero. It's a good place to break your journey and have a snack.
■ Between 10 and 20 October every year, the **Festival del Bailador Rumbero** is held at Matanzas' Teatro Sauto.

At Your Leisure

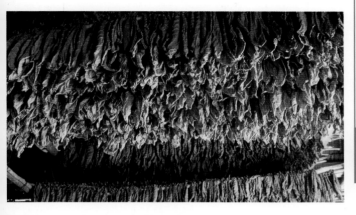

Cuba's finest tobacco leaves drying in a hut in Vuelta Abajo

4 Vuelta Abajo

Cuba is well-known as the source of the world's finest cigars, and it has long been acknowledged that the very finest cigar tobacco comes from the district of Vuelta Abajo. This fertile valley around the small town of San Juan y Martínez, just 22km (14 miles) southwest of Pinar del Río, is well worth a half-day's visit. The secret of Vuelta Abajo lies in the richness of the red soil, which is well-watered but (crucially) quite dry during the tobacco-growing season.

Green fields of tobacco leaves cover the region, many protected by cloth from direct sunlight, while tobacco-drying sheds, where leaves are hung to cure, can be seen everywhere. Head for Finca Pinar San Luís, where the son of legendary Alejandro Robaina will gladly show you around his renowned tobacco farm, which has been in his family for generations. Robaina, who died in 2010 at the age of 91, was acknowledged as Cuba's main ambassador of cigars. Guided tours are offered, and there's a lounge with memorabilia about Robaina's many meetings with world leaders.

➕ 178 B3

Finca Pinar San Luís
✉ Near San Juan y Martínez ☎ (48) 797470
🕓 Mon–Sat 9–5

5 Soroa

Soroa is a lush hill resort snuggling in the hills of the Sierra del Rosario just 75km (47 miles) southwest of Havana. It's close enough to the capital to make it an ideal weekend retreat, and during the early years of the Cuban Revolution it was popular with the communist élite. Today, it serves a wider clientele. The main resort, Hotel and Villa Horizontes Soroa, offers accommodation in cabins set around a pool, as well as hiking, horse-riding and birdwatching tours. There's also a fine orchid garden with more than 300 species, but the most popular sight is the Salto del Arco Iris, a small, attractive waterfall with a cool swimming area. Be warned, though – after violent rains the falls become dangerously powerful, and swimming is not recommended.

➕ 179 D4

Salto del Arco Iris
🎟 Moderate; free if you stay at Villa Soroa

6 Varadero

Varadero – more precisely the long and narrow Punta Hicacos Peninsula – is Cuba's primary tourist resort and the nearest thing that you'll find to Spain's Costa del Sol. The entire peninsula is given over to tourism, with most hotels specializing in all-in packages. Tourist flights direct from Europe and Canada arrive at the international airport, just 6km (3.7 miles) off the main road between Matanzas and Varadero.

Varadero has its good points and its bad, but it's certainly not the real Cuba. Most Cubans are forbidden access to the peninsula unless they have employment there (with wages of around US$1 a day, be sure to tip if you do stay here). Private hotels and restaurants are banned by the state. Most types of watersport are available, and the seas are warm, safe and clean. Skydiving is a popular activity. Otherwise, there's little to see and do, and food remains a weak link, except at the all-in resorts. If you're on a two-week package to soak up the sun, it may be the best place on the island.

🞢 180 A4 ✈ Juan Gualberto Gómez International Airport

7 Cárdenas

If you're staying in Varadero and want to experience the real Cuba, then Cárdenas is the easiest and most natural place to go. Just 18km (11 miles) southeast of Varadero along a good (if narrow) road, it's quintessentially Cuban. There's not much to the town, which has a population of about 100,000 inhabitants, many of whom work in the nearby resort of Varadero. There's an old, run-down shipyard, a rum factory and the usual sugar mills dotted around the countryside surrounding the town.

But Cárdenas does have atmosphere. Built on an easy-to-follow grid pattern, the town's focal point is the Catedral de la Immaculada Concepción (c.1850), a fine old church noted for its stained-glass windows and fronted by a statue of Christopher Columbus, which was sculpted by the Spanish artist Piquier in 1862. There's also an unusual cast-iron market called Plaza Molocoff, dating from 1859, with a 16m-high (53-foot) dome, which is worth taking a look at. The main draw is the Museo Oscar María de Rojas, housed in the former town

Colourful houses line the narrow streets of Cárdenas

hall and exhibiting fabulous mementoes recalling Cuba's colonial and revolutionary past. This is not only one of the country's longest standing museums, but also one of its most impressive.

➕ 180 A4

Museo Oscar María de Rojas
✉ Avenida 4 Este y Calle 12 ☎ (45) 522417 🕐 Tue–Sat 9–6, Sun 9–1 💰 Moderate

🎱 Península de Zapata

Most of southern Matanzas Province is given over to the sugar fields, swamps and the wetlands of the Zapata Peninsula. The area is easily accessed via the *autopista* from Havana to Santa Clara. Take a right turn at Jagüey Grande and you'll be heading right into the heart of Zapata.

Most of the 4,500sq km (1,755sq mile) peninsula is now included in the Grand Parque Natural Montemar, which has been declared a UNESCO biosphere reserve. The whole area is a prime destination for birdwatchers, anglers and nature lovers of all kinds. It's also one of the few places where you will have a good chance of seeing a Cuban manatee. Las Salinas Wildlife Refuge is famous for the tens of thousands of pink flamingos that congregate here between October and April. Nature aside, Zapata is also the location of the "Bay of Pigs" (➤ this page), site of the CIA-sponsored Cuban mercenary invasion defeated by Castro in 1961.

About 18km (11 miles) south of Central Australia, an Indian village supposedly based on the habitations and lifestyles of the pre-Columbian Taíno Indians has been re-created. The 20-minute boat trip through the Zapata marshes to La Boca de Guamá is well worthwhile, both for the wildlife, including crocodiles, flamingos and ibis, and for a rare chance to learn something, however spurious, about Cuba's original indigenous population.

➕ 179 E3

La Boca de Guamá
✉ 18km (11 miles) south of Jagüey Grande

Hutia inhabit the swamplands of Zapata

☎ (45) 912458 🚌 40-minute roundtrip through the Laguna del Tesoro 💰 Expensive

🎱 Bahía de Cochinos

From La Boca, the road continues south to the Bahía de Cochinos (Bay of Pigs), site of the infamous CIA invasion. Just why the US intelligence services and their Cuban allies should have decided on this bay as a landing place remains obscure – it's a long way from anywhere of importance, easily isolated, and surrounded by very difficult, marshy countryside. Today, the Bay of Pigs is an area of natural beauty, with a gorgeous beach melding into the Caribbean Sea.

Playa Larga, at the head of the bay, is a base for scuba diving. To the east, the road follows the shore of the bay past numerous good diving and snorkelling points, the best of which is Cueva de los Peces, a well-signposted cenote, or flooded fault in the earth's surface, that is more than 70m (230ft) deep. Isolated, cool and with a restaurant next door, it's an excellent place for a break and a meal. The snorkelling in the nearby sea is also highly recommended.

➕ 180 A5

Cueva de los Peces
🕐 Daily 9–5 💰 Free

⑩ Playa Girón

Beyond Cueva de los Peces, the road swings east, still hugging the coast, to reach the isolated resort of Playa Girón. There's a beautiful (if largely deserted) beach, mired by a concrete breakwater built to thwart a possible second CIA-sponsored invasion. Developed for international tourism, the beach is now off-limits to local Cuban residents, and the Hotel Playa Girón is used by package holidaymakers and Latin American medical patients. There's good snorkelling and swimming, as well as the Museo de Girón, displaying trophies commemorating Castro's triumph over the invaders.

A farther 8km (5 miles) away at Caleta Buena, you'll find splendid snorkelling in a lovely cove. Here, there's an International Scuba Center that specializes in guiding divers through a series of underwater caves populated with sightless fish.
✚ 180 A3

Museo de Girón
✉ Opposite Villa Playa Girón, Playa Girón
☎ (45) 984122 🕒 Daily 8–5 💲 Inexpensive

A solitary swimmer in the intense blue waters is framed by palm trees at Playa Girón

Where to...
Stay

Prices
Expect to pay per double room per night:
$ under CUC50 $$ CUC50–150 $$$ over CUC150

MATANZAS

Islazul Hotel Canimao $$

There are no hotels in Matanzas, except some mediocre private room rentals. There are many fine options, including all-inclusives, available in the nearby resort of Varadero (▶92). Otherwise, your only choice is the Islazul Hotel Canimao, 8km (5 miles) east of town on the Matanzas–Varadero highway. This Soviet-era hotel has pleasantly decorated rooms with satellite TVs, security boxes and modern bathrooms with hair-dryers. The Tropicana nightclub adjoins the hotel, which has a small bar and restaurant.

➕ 179 F4 ☒ Via Blanca, Canimao
☎ (45) 253429; www.islazul.cu

NUEVA GERONA

Villa Isla de la Juventud $

Probably the best hotel – certainly the most congenial – in Nueva Gerona, Villa Isla de la Juventud is near the airport and has fine views across the island, especially at sunset. The staff are friendly and welcoming, and the rooms have cool marble underfoot and mini-fridges (Nueva Gerona can become pretty humid in summer). However, the restaurant is not particularly great, and loud music often blasts from the area around the swimming pool until well into the evening, particularly at weekends. If you're not into disco and partying, be sure to ask for a room well away from the pool.

➕ 179 D3 ☒ Autopista Nueva Gerona–Santa Fe Km1 ☎ (45) 323290

PINAR DEL RÍO

Hotel Vuelta Abajo $$

This colonial-era hotel went into decline following the Revolution and was abandoned. It reopened after a complete restoration that has rekindled much of its former charm. The airy lobby has precious antiques, and a marble staircase spirals up to the hotel's 24 rooms, appointed with simple antique furnishings. High ceilings help to keep the heat at bay, although rooms facing the streets can be rather noisy. Although nothing to write home about, the restaurant here is the best in town, and the hotel also has a tour desk and internet access.

➕ 178 C3 ☒ Calle Martí Oeste 103
☎ (48) 759381; www.islazul.cu

PLAYA LARGA

Horizontes Playa Larga $

The Horizontes is another offering from the state-run agency, Cubanacán. It is a decent, no-frills option, a good choice for nature-lovers wanting to explore the unspoiled surroundings for a few days. The spacious chalets include a lounge area, with TVs, although the restaurant serves poor food and leaves a lot to be desired. The main draw is the hotel's beautiful, beachfront location, and peaceful, relaxing atmosphere – few visitors stay in this area, other than dedicated fishing enthusiasts and keen birdwatchers.

➕ 179 F3 ☒ Peninsula de Zapata
☎ (45) 987212; www.hotelescubanacan.com

SOROA

Hotel and Villa Horizontes Soroa $$

In the hills above Candeleria, the setting of this hotel is the main reason to stay. Somewhat down at heel and basic accommodation consists of bungalows overlooking a swimming pool with sunbathing facilities and a poolside bar. The hotel has an adequate restaurant that is open to non-guests. Staying here entitles guests to free entry to the nearby orchidarium, as well as the Salto del Arco Iris waterfall. The friendly staff speak English.

🛈 179 D4 🖾 Carretera de Soroa Km8, Candelaria 🕾 (85) 3534

VARADERO

Barceló Marina Palace Resort $$$

Of the scores of all-inclusive resorts in Varadero, this one is still one of the nicest, although it is a considerable distance from town at the very tip of the peninsula. Its spectacular setting behind sand dunes is matched by the gorgeous decor, playing on a maritime theme. The 300 junior suites and suites have beautiful furnishings and state-of-the-art amenities, plus there's a choice of quality restaurants, nightly entertainment and plenty of watersports. You can also enjoy a large pool with spiral waterslide.

🛈 180 A5 🖾 Punta Hicacos final, Varadero 🕾 (45) 669966; www.barcelomarinapalace.com

Internacional $$$

A long-standing Varadero favourite, this hotel first opened in 1950 as a twin to Miami's Hotel Fontainbleau and has since been restored. Its views from the top floors. There's a swimming pool and tennis courts, cabaret and disco, several bars and two restaurants, both serving good international and *criollo* (Creole) fare. The friendly staff can't seem to do enough for their guests – just don't forget to tip. Car rental and money exchange facilities can be found in the main lobby. English is well spoken by the desk staff, and menus are in English and Spanish.

🛈 180 A5 🖾 Avenida de las Américas, Varadero 🕾 (45) 667038; www.hotel-varaderointernacional.com

Islazul Dos Mares $

This reasonably priced, clean, albeit no-frills hotel is just 100m (110 yards) from the beach, with simply appointed rooms, a good bar and an attached restaurant. Dos Mares offers good value and great access both to the sea and to nearby restaurants and night spots. The service can be a bit cool, however. Prices include breakfast. There's an unguarded parking area on Calle 53 outside the main entrance.

🛈 180 A5 🖾 Avenida 1 and Calle 53, Varadero 🕾 (45) 612702; www.islazul.cu

Mansion Xanadu $$$

The most atmospheric of the many hotels in Varadero, this one is the former mansion of chemical magnate Irénee Du Pont. Exuding historic charm, it is flush with antiques, carved mahogany fixtures and ornate Moorish tilework. Marble floors gleam in the six bedrooms with huge marble showers. The restaurant is one of Varadero's best, and there's live music nightly. Plus, golfers can tee off right outside the door, and the beach is just steps away.

🛈 180 A5 🖾 Avenida de las Américas, Varadero 🕾 (45) 668482; www.varaderogolfclub.com

Sol Palmeras $$$

One of the original all-inclusives, this huge hotel is a joint venture between Cubanacán and the giant Spanish Sol Meliá chain. The foreign management shows, as service is well above average. There are more than 400 rooms and 200 bungalows arranged around a large swimming pool close to the beach. Amenities include numerous bars, restaurants, money exchange,

Where to...
Eat and Drink

Prices

Expect to pay per person for a two-course meal, excluding drinks and service:

$ under CUC10 $$ CUC10–25 $$$ over CUC25

VIÑALES

La Ermita $$

Viñales' best, La Ermita is about 2km (1.2 miles) east of the small town on a hilltop with fine views. Facilities include tennis, swimming and horse-riding. The restaurant provides simple but good food, and the hotel is within walking distance of Viñales' main street and numerous other eateries. The view across Viñales Valley (▶154) is breathtaking.

➕ 178 C4 ✉ Carretera a La Ermita Km1.5 ☎ (8) 796071; www.hotel-la-ermita-cuba.com

NUEVA GERONA

Restaurante El Dragón $

This establishment specializes in Chinese cuisine – though the choice is limited and not very sophisticated. Nevertheless, it's reasonably priced, clean and the food is filling – and it's a welcome change to find the (usually excellent) Cuban pork prepared in a "sweet and sour" sauce rather than just grilled, fried or stewed. Staff strike a gong as you enter, and there's music – Cuban, not Chinese – after 7:30 in the evenings. Other Cuban-Chinese dishes on the menu (but not necessarily always available) include chop suey and spring rolls. There are also numerous criollo staples – but the decor seems authentically Chinese, at least by Nueva Gerona standards.

➕ 179 D3 ✉ Calles 39 and 26 ☎ (46) 324479 ⏰ Daily 12–10

PINAR DEL RÍO

Rumayor $$

Pinar del Río's main government restaurant is 1km (0.6 miles) north of town, just off the road to Viñales. This Polynesian-style restaurant (the decor is a carry-over from the 1950s) serves reasonable criollo fare as well as a couple of more unusual dishes, pollo ahumado (smoked chicken) and caldosa puerco (stewed pork). The latter is relatively hard to find on up-country menus, but with Moros y Cristianos (black beans and rice), it's nourishing and tasty. Rumayor often has a cabaret show (Thu–Sun) in a large outdoor amphitheatre featuring Cuba's Afro-Caribbean dance and music. Admission costs an extra CUC5, but the ticket comes with one free drink.

➕ 178 C3 ✉ Carretera Pinar del Río–Viñales Km1 ☎ (82) 763007 ⏰ Daily 12–12

SOROA

Hotel and Villa Horizontes Soroa $$

Soroa is a hill resort; there's no town, so there isn't a great deal of choice in places to eat. In fact, there's really only one worth considering, and that's the restaurant attached to this hotel. pharmacy, car rentals and tennis courts. The choice of food available is unusually extensive for Cuba, with international and Italian cuisine topping the menu. There's also a rudimentary business centre with email services.

➕ 180 A5 ✉ Carretera de las Morlas, Autopista Sur Km9, Varadero ☎ (45) 667009; www.solmelia.com

restaurant. It's unusually good for a Cuban government-run hotel, offering a really exceptional buffet that includes a wide selection of *criollo* pork, chicken and beef dishes, along with local soups and salads. There are desserts such as crème caramel and cream cake in addition to more healthy options of fresh sliced pineapple and watermelon. There's a reasonable wine list, too – perhaps reflecting the fact that Villa Soroa served for many years as a retreat for the Cuban communist elite.

+ 179 D4 **⊠** Carretera de Soroa Km8, Candelaria **☎** (85) 3534 **⊙** Daily 7–9.45

VARADERO

Antigüedades $$

One of the most upscale restaurants in Varadero outside the all-inclusive resorts, this elegant eatery on the main drag adjoining Parque Josones, is adorned throughout with antiques, old prints, original paintings and various photos of Hollywood's greatest, plus posters from their well-known films. Even the place settings comprise real silverware and porcelain – a rarity for Cuba. The restaurant specializes in filet mignon and lobster dishes, but the menu also offers a wide range of continental dishes. Quality surpasses that of most restaurants in town, and the service from the crisply dressed waiters is usually sharp and professional.

+ 180 A5 **⊠** Avenida 1ra and Calle 59 **☎** (45) 667329 **⊙** Daily 12–11

Casa de Fondue $$

The "House of Fondue" serves much more than just fondue dishes. Its menu, which is French-Swiss inspired with a good number of international dishes, includes almost everything from prawn cocktail and steak to lobster – and, of course, the eponymous fondue. Recently refurbished, Casa de Fondue is a good-value restaurant that is particularly popular with hotel guests taking a break from their all-inclusive standard international hotel meals.

+ 180 A5 **⊠** Avenida 1ra and Calle 63 **☎** (45) 667747 **⊙** Daily 12–11

El Bodegón Criollo $$

The name tells the story – *criollo* cuisine, but in this case unusually well prepared and more varied than most. Seafood is, understandably, the house speciality, and the lobster is as fresh as you could wish for and quite excellent. The flame-grilled, succulent burgers are pretty good and the bread rolls are soft and palatable, unusual for Cuba where the bread is often hard. If you like your burgers spicy, bring your own salsa – jars are readily available in most Varadero supermarkets, but for some reason they don't often appear on restaurant dining tables.

+ 180 A5 **⊠** Avenida de la Playa and Calle 40 **☎** (45) 667784 **⊙** Daily 12–11

Lai Lai $$

Another of Cuba's Chinese restaurants, Lai Lai's cuisine is inevitably partly *criollo* – though because this is Varadero rather than just any provincial town, the choice of dishes is more authentic and varied than in most Sino-Cuban places. The ambience is studiously Chinese (though the oriental characters depicted on the entrance doors are artistic licence, and not Chinese script). Choose between sitting at tables or dining cross-legged on the floor. The restaurant shuts early for Varadero, so don't leave it too late.

+ 180 A5 **⊠** Avenida 1ra and Calle 18 **☎** (45) 667793 **⊙** Daily 12:30–9.30

El Mesón del Quijote $$$

Upmarket says it all. You can tell this by the setting, in a castle-like tower on top of a low mound by the Avenida de las Américas – just look for the metallic statues of Don Quixote, Sancho Panza and their donkey. The cuisine is appropriately Andalusian, and there's an extremely reasonable wine list featuring, especially, Spanish wines.

Reservations are recommended, particularly at weekends.

☐ 180 A5 ☒ Avenida de las Américas and Calle B Las Morlas ☎ (45) 667796 ⏰ Daily 12–12

VIÑALES

La Casa de Don Tomás $$

Viñales' best government restaurant can be found in an old colonial mansion that has character and an outside balcony for alfresco dining, although it tends to be popular with tour groups so can get busy. The dish to look for is *las delicias de Don Tomás*, consisting of a selection of lobster, fish, pork, chicken and sausage served with *arroz blanco* (white rice). Other fare on offer includes fried chicken and pork steaks, various seafood dishes sometimes including fresh lobster, *papas fritas* (fries) and chilled Cuban beer. Musicians usually provide the entertainment.

☐ 178 C4 ☒ Salvador Cisneros 140 ☎ (8) 796300 ⏰ Daily 10–9:30

Where to... Shop

Despite its proximity to the capital city, Cuba west of Havana has few shopping opportunities apart from the ubiquitous cigars and rum. The provincial capitals of Pinar del Río and Matanzas have fallen on hard times. That they were once prosperous is obvious from the 19th-century architecture and the local museums, but there's an almost complete lack of hard-currency stores and even peso shops are poorly stocked. By contrast, east of Matanzas is relatively well-stocked Varadero, with goods catering for hard-currency tourists.

CIGARS

It is generally agreed that the Pinar del Río district of Vuelta Abajo (▶ 87) grows the finest cigar tobacco in the world, and no visitor to Pinar should miss the Fábrica de Tabacos Francisco Donatién (▶ 79, 80), where cigars of unusual excellence are for sale.

RUM

Pinar has its own unique rum, *Guayabita del Pinar*, which is found nowhere else in the world and makes a distinctive and reasonably priced souvenir. It's for sale at the Fábrica de Bebidas Guayabita (▶ 78, 80). There are two varieties, dry and sweet, both of them rated at around 40 per cent alcohol. In Varadero, **La Casa de Ron**, at Avenida 1ra, esq 63, stocks more than 100 rum labels, including rare aged *añejos*.

SOUVENIRS

The main street in **Viñales**, especially the square by the Iglesia Viñales, has souvenir stalls selling all manner of knick-knacks, T-shirts and revolutionary memorabilia.

Isolated Archipiélago de los Canarreos is virtually devoid of shopping opportunities, but **Cayo Largo** has government-owned outlets at the major hotels selling apparatus for basic watersports.

For a real souvenir-shopping spree, however, you can't beat the major malls and tourist hotels of **Varadero**, which you'll find every few hundred yards. Several street markets all sell a similar range of craft souvenirs – tiny wooden drums, papier mâché antique cars, lace blouses, etc. Quality ceramics can be bought at the **Taller de Cerámica Artística**, at Avenida 1 and Calle 59.

In **Matanzas**, be sure to watch for the hand-crafted books at Ediciones Vigía (▶ 84, 86).

Where to...
Be Entertained

Western Cuba (beyond the City of Havana) can really be divided into three distinct entertainment zones – Varadero, the Archipiélago de los Canarreos, and the rest. In the far west, Pinar del Río Province has very little nightlife and few cabarets, and the same is true of Matanzas Province and nearly all of Matanzas. In Varadero, by contrast, nightlife abounds while both Varadero and Archipiélago de los Canarreos are all about watersports.

THE ARTS

The arts in Pinar del Río are represented by the **Teatro José Jacinto Milanés**, at Calle Martí, a fine old institution featuring weekly musical recitals and theatrical productions, and by the **Casa de la Música**, at Calle Gerardo Medina, which stages folkloric dances.

In Matanzas, the **Teatro Sala José White** on Calle 79, presents regular classical concerts and jazz evenings. The better-known **Teatro Sauto**, at Plaza de la Vigía (▶84) holds classical concerts on Friday to Sunday evenings. There's a **Casa de la Cultura**, at Calle 272, which organizes poetry readings and theatrical shows.

In the Archipiélago de los Canarreos, there's a **Casa de la Cultura**, at Nueva Gerona Calle 37.

NIGHTLIFE

In Matanzas, the **Ruinas de Matasiete** by the mouth of the Río San Juan is a lively bar named after a local bandit. In Nueva Gerona, try **Casa de los Vinos**, at Calle 41. In Cayo Largo del Sur, most nightlife revolves around the all-inclusive hotels with their own bars and nightclubs on site.

DISCOS

The only disco in Pinar del Río is **Disco Azul**, at Hotel Pinar on Gonzales Alcorta (closed Mondays). Matanzas has no disco, but **El Pescadito**, at Calle 272, is a lively, local bar. Varadero overflows with discos and dance clubs – try **La Comparsita**, at Calle 60, the **Club Nocturno Havana Club**, at Calle 62 final, and **Casa de la Música** at Calle 42, with live bands.

CABARET

In Pinar del Río, there's a cabaret at Rumayor (▶93). Matanzas boasts an open-air spectacular, the **Cabaret Tropicana**, outside town at Canimao – it's one of the top three cabarets in Cuba.

Nueva Gerona's **Cabaret el Patio**, at Calle 24, is open Thursday to Sunday. There are several cabarets in Varadero, the largest of which is **Cabaret Continental** at the Hotel Internacional on Avenida las Américas, while pirate-themed **La Cueva del Pirata** is set in a natural cave at Autopista Sur, Km 11.

SPORTS

The Bahía de Corrientes, in western Pinar del Río, offers superb diving at **María la Gorda International Dive Center**. Scuba diving can be arranged by **Puertosol International Diving Center**, at the Hotel El Colony on the Ensenada de la Siguanea.

On Cayo Largo del Sur, the various all-in hotels offer a large choice of watersports, and there's a dive shop at Playa Sirena.

Varadero offers a wide range of snorkelling, scuba diving, windsurfing, sailing, kayaking, deep-sea fishing and skydiving.

Central Cuba

Getting Your Bearings

To many visitors, central Cuba may seem a necessary (if convenient) corridor between Havana and the culturally more exciting east of the country. Nevertheless, it does have much to offer, including the sophisticated and cultured cities of Cienfuegos and Camagüey, as well as the twin architectural jewels of Remedios and Trinidad. The central towns of Santa Clara, Sancti Spíritus and Ciego de Ávila are pleasant, but have little to offer in the way of classical architecture and other attractions, although Santa Clara has the excellent Museo de Che.

Baños de Elguea
Corralillo
Isabela de Sagua
Alturas del Norte
Sagua la Grande
Cayo Fragoso
Presa Alacranes
Emilio Córdova
CC
Mordazo
CN
Cifuentes
Encrucijada
Santo Domingo
Hatillo
VILLA CLARA
Camajuaní
Caibarién
Bahía B
9 **Remedios**
A1
Esperanza
8 **Santa Clara**
Cartagena
Lajas
Ranchuelo
CC
Alturas
Aguada de Pasajeros
Cruces
San Juan de los Yeras
Alturas de Santa Clara
Placetas
CC
Iguar
Rodas
A1
CIENFUEGOS
Palmira
Manicaragua
Fomento
Cabaiguán
Yaguaramas
Caunao
Cienfuegos **1**
Jardín Botánico Soledad **5**
Presa del Hanabanilla
Sancti Spíritus
Taguas
Zaza
Castillo de Jagua **4**
Playa Rancho Luna
1150m▲
Pico San Juan
Macizo de Guamuhaya
842m▲ Loma de Banao
Jati
Presa Zaza
Parque Natural Topes de Collantes
Topes de Collantes
Trinidad **2** **7** **Valle de los Ingenios**
CS
Banao
SANCTI SPÍRITUS
Playa Ancón **6**
Casilda
Guasimal
Playa Tayabacoa
Tunas de Zaza

Away from the central spine – the *Carretera Central* (Central Highway) and the main railway line linking Havana with Santiago de Cuba, as well as the uncompleted *autopista*, which peters out just north of Jatibonico – it's another matter altogether. The northern coast of central Cuba is distinguished by the Jardines del Rey (Gardens of the King),

a long, lush range of tropical cays just offshore, many now easily accessible by massive causeways, offering some of the best beach resorts on the island. The same is true of the southern coast, where the more distant Jardines de la Reina (Gardens of the Queen) are less accessible and less developed. Then there's the Sierra del Escambray (► 159–161), an almost untouristed range of saw-toothed mountains between Cienfuegos and Trinidad, offering one of the best drives on the island.

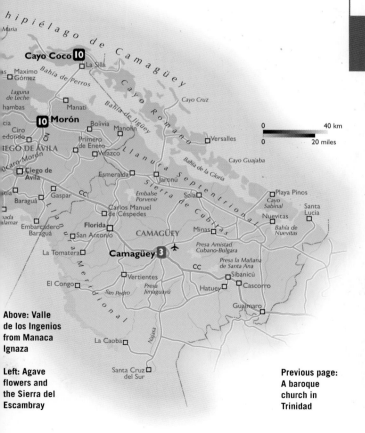

Above: Valle de los Ingenios from Manaca Ignaza

Left: Agave flowers and the Sierra del Escambray

Previous page: A baroque church in Trinidad

In Three Days

If you're not quite sure where to begin your travels, this itinerary recommends three practical and enjoyable days out in central Cuba, taking in some of the best places to see using the Getting Your Bearings map on the previous page. For more information, see the main entries.

Day 1

Morning
Rise early and explore 🚩**Cienfuegos'** (➤ 102–105) central Parque José Martí area before heading to the southern part of town to visit the Palacio de Valle (below; ➤ 104). After lunch at this remarkable restaurant, head off to the nearby 🚩**Jardín Botánico Soledad** (➤ 114).

Afternoon
Drive along the coast in the lee of the beautiful **Sierra del Escambray** (➤ 159–161), arriving in 🚩**Trinidad** (opposite; ➤ 106–109) with time to explore the cobbled plazas.

Evening
After enjoying what is usually a golden sunset, relax with a meal in one of the bars or restaurants around Parque Céspedes (➤ 107).

Day 2

Morning
After further exploration of **2 Trinidad's** streets, visit nearby **7 Playa Ancón** (➤ 114–115) for a swim, then head east to the **8 Valle de los Ingenios** (➤ 115–116) and Manaca Iznaga (➤ 116), half an hour east of Trinidad.

Afternoon
Continue northeast, pausing for lunch in Sancti Spíritus at the Mesón de la Plaza (➤ 121) on Parque Honorato. You now have the choice of heading north to the medieval town of **9 Remedios** (➤ 117) or turning east along the *Carretera Central* to historic **3 Camagüey** (➤ 110–113).

Evening
If you chose **Remedios**, enjoy dinner and overnight at the historic Hotel Mascotte (➤ 119). If you opt for Camagüey, dine and stay in the fine Hotel Colón (➤ 118).

Day 3

Morning
After exploring Remedios, drive northeast via the fishing port of Caibarién to take the causeway to the beach resort of Cayo Santa María. If in Camagüey, explore the old city around Plaza de los Trabajadores, Plaza San Juan de Dios, Plaza Carmen and Parque Agramonte.

Afternoon
At Cayo Santa María, sunbathe, swim and relax. From Camagüey, drive north through **10 Morón** to **Cayo Coco** (➤ 117) for some idyllic relaxation, arriving in time for sunset and the sight of flamingos in flight.

Evening
Enjoy a rest by the sea and a good meal at the Meliá Cayo Coco resort (➤ 118), or the Villa Las Brujas (➤ 118) on Cayo Santa María.

❶ Cienfuegos

With more than 180,000 inhabitants, Cienfuegos is a
large city by Cuban standards. It's also of great strategic
importance, located on the east side of the beautiful Bahía
de Cienfuegos, possibly Cuba's finest natural harbour. The
strategic significance of the bay was recognized long before
the city was built. Because the area was unsettled but the bay
sheltered and secure, it developed into a haven for pirates,
obliging the Spanish authorities to build a fortress, the
Castillo de Jagua (➤ 114), at the western mouth of the bay in
the early 18th century to deny them access.

It wasn't until the late 18th century that serious settlement
began in Cienfuegos itself. The first colonists came from
Bordeaux in France, infusing a distinct architectural style on
the early city. Many French refugees from the 1791 revolution
in Haiti, when the black slave leader Toussaint Louverture
overthrew French rule, also fled to Cienfuegos as a place
of refuge and resettlement. Then came French refugees

Springtime in Parque José Martí, fronting the cathedral

from Louisiana after Napoleon sold the territory to the US in 1803, further reinforcing the French connection. As a consequence, many Cubans claim that the people of Cienfuegos have a higher percentage of blonde hair and blue eyes than elsewhere in the island. Regardless, there is a palpably French feel to some of the city's parks, tree-lined boulevards and buildings.

The Historic Heart

Cienfuegos is built on a grid pattern, which makes it easy to find your way about. The main north–south boulevard is **Paseo del Prado**, running from the city's southernmost tip at Punta Gorda through the heart of town to the main road to Havana in the north. The oldest and most interesting part of town lies astride and a little to the west of Paseo del Prado, and is focused on **Parque José Martí**, a shrine to the national hero whose white marble statue dominates the park.

Parque José Martí, one of the finest municipal parks anywhere in the country, is the best place to begin any exploration of Cienfuegos, not least because the square is dominated by so many distinguished buildings, but also because **Avenue 54**, leading east from the park to Paseo del Prado, is an attractive walkway.

On the east side of the park stands the neoclassical **Catedral de la Purísima Concepción**, built in 1869 and distinguished by two fine towers and imported French stained-glass windows featuring the 12 apostles. It's worth entering to view its Corinthian altar and high vaulted ceiling, which makes it cool during the heat of midday. Outside, facing the shaded square and the statue of José Martí, are two white marble lions. To the north of the square is the renowned **Teatro Tomás Terry**, built in 1899 to seat an audience of 950 in an Italian-style auditorium constructed of Cuban cedar. Famous performers who appeared here in the theatre's heyday include Sarah Bernhardt, Enrico Caruso and Anna Pavlova. The theatre remains an elegant neoclassical building and one of the architectural gems of Cienfuegos, where performances by Cuba's national ballet and opera companies still regularly take place (➤ 123).

Art and Music

Continuing round the square in a counterclockwise direction, the next distinguished building is the neoclassical **Colegio San Lorenzo**. West of the square is the **Casa de la Cultura Benjamin Duarte**, in the Palacio Ferrer – a building with an impressive cupola and a tower, which may be ascended for fine views over the town and bay for a small tip.

A further row of distinguished buildings on the south side of the square completes Cienfuegos' Parque José Martí. These include the **Museo Provincial**, displaying a wide selection of items dating from pre-Columbian times to the bourgeois trappings of life in late colonial Cienfuegos, and the **Galería Maroya** art gallery.

Away from the Heart of Town

Away from central Cienfuegos, the city's most extraordinary site is the Moorish-style **Palacio de Valle**, at the southern end of Paseo del Prado, in the formerly upmarket district of Punta Gorda. This unusual building – which would seem more in place in Seville or Tangiers than in Cienfuegos – was commissioned in 1913 by a local businessman, Aciclio de Valle y Blanco, who employed skilled craftsmen from Morocco to construct a Moorish palace in authentic style. Unlike the central *kiosko* (bandstand) in Manzanillo (➤ 140), the Arabic text recurring in and around the murals of the Palacio de Valle is authentic and well-executed. Today, the Palacio functions as a seafood restaurant and small museum. A speciality of the palace is the out-of-tune piano and show put on by Carmen, a friendly if flamboyant transvestite who wears elaborate "Arabian" style dress.

One further historical monument worthy of a visit is the **Cementerio La Reina** (Queen's Cemetery), way out in the west of town on a small peninsula projecting into Cienfuegos Bay. Established in 1837, this extravagant but rundown cemetery is notable for the numerous marble graves of Spanish soldiers who died during the wars of Cuban independence.

The elaborate Moorish-style Palacio de Valle

Colegio San Lorenzo, one of the fine buildings bordering Parque José Martí

For a more contemporary sobering experience and *memento mori*, raise your eyes and look west. In the distance, across the beautiful bay, a huge concrete dome can be seen on the horizon. This is the unfinished **Jaragua Nuclear Power Plant**, begun in cooperation with the Soviet authorities in 1982, which was to produce around 10 per cent of Cuba's electrical generating capacity. Work stalled in 1990 with the collapse of the Soviet Union and is still at a standstill. Not all Cienfuegans seem dismayed, however – "that might have been Cuba's Chernobyl" is a common (if discreet) view held by locals.

TAKING A BREAK

Try the Palacio de Valle (➤ 121) or one of the coffee shops to the east of Parque José Martí.

✚ 180 B3

Catedral de la Purísima Concepción
✉ Avenida 56 ☎ (43) 525 297
🕐 Daily 8–3 💷 Free

Teatro Tomás Terry
✉ Avenida 56 and Calle 27
☎ (43) 513361 🕐 Daily 9–6
💷 Inexpensive

Museo Provincial
✉ Avenida 54 and Calle 27
☎ (43) 519722 🕐 Tue–Sat 10–6,
Sun 9–12 💷 Inexpensive

Galería Maroya
✉ Avenida 54 and Calle 27
🕐 Mon–Sat 9–6, Sun 9–1
💷 Free

CIENFUEGOS: INSIDE INFO

Top tips A number of agencies offer **city tours** of Cienfuegos (often combined with Trinidad) from Havana and Varadero; such as Cuba Excursions (www.cubaexcursions.com), or enquire at your hotel.
■ **Boat trips** around the bay and deep-sea fishing tours can be arranged with Marina Marlin Cienfuegos (Calle 35 e/ 6 and 8, Reparto Punta Gorda, tel: (43) 556120, www.nauticamarlin.com).

Hidden gem Every other year in September, the **Benny Moré International Festival of Popular Music** takes place in various venues around town.

2 Trinidad

The small settlement of Trinidad, nestled in the lee of the Sierra del Escambray, ranks as the most authentically medieval town in Cuba. This was recognized even before the Cuban Revolution, during the time of the dictator Batista, as in the mid-1950s Trinidad was officially declared a "National Monument" and any unauthorized new construction was forbidden. This sensible policy was reinforced in 1988 when both Trinidad and the nearby Valle de los Ingenios (▶ 115–116) were declared World Heritage Sites by UNESCO.

Trinidad – really little more than a large village with a population of around 40,000 – was founded by Diego Velázquez in 1514 as Cuba's third European colonial settlement. Initially, it prospered as a gold-mining hub, and also as a base of operations for the conquistador Hernán Cortés (▶ 13) during his 1518 invasion and conquest of Mexico. Subsequently, Havana suceeded Trinidad as the main base for Spanish operations against the Central American mainland, but by this time sugar cane grown in the fertile soil around Trinidad was already replacing locally mined gold as the town's main source of wealth.

From Sugar Trade to Tourism

During the 18th century, Trinidad and the nearby Valle de los Ingenios entered their boom period. Fortunes were made,

Looking over the rooftops of Trinidad to the Sierra del Escambray

fine buildings, both religious and secular, were constructed, and the town acquired an elegant dignity, which still survives, despite years of isolation and poverty after the local sugar industry fell into decline by the late 18th century. Trinidad – one of the most popular destinations beyond Havana – is experiencing its third period of economic prosperity, as tourists flock to admire this unique and remarkably well-preserved historic gem.

Trinidad is tucked into foothills that rise northwest into the Sierra del Escambray (➤ 159–161). It rises perceptibly upwards away from the sea towards the old town centre, a warren of charmingly irregular streets and plazas cobbled in a very rough fashion, with uneven blocks of stone sloping inwards to a central gutter. Local legend has it that the first mayor had one leg shorter than the other and designed the town in this fashion to facilitate his getting around, but it used to be pretty standard town drainage in the Middle Ages.

Exploring Trinidad

Most visitors entering Trinidad will head for the south-central **Parque Céspedes**, where the main hotels and restaurants are located. It's best to stay here and walk uphill and inland to the **Plaza Mayor**, which is the historic heart of old Trinidad. Simple, pastel-hued houses with red shingle-tiled roofs and elaborate window grilles line every street, often with older residents sitting on the porch in rocking chairs just watching time pass.

It takes about 20 minutes to reach Plaza Mayor from Parque Céspedes. Plaza Mayor is a delightful shaded square surrounded by colonial buildings. It's especially glorious at sunset on a clear day, when the facades of the ancient buildings glow like hammered gold from the auburn sunlight slanting in from the south.

A Town of Churches

Plaza Mayor is dominated to the north (uphill) by the **Iglesia Parroquial de la Santísima Trinidad**. The baroque front is magnificent, and inside is a venerated statue, *Christ of the True Cross,* in the heart of an altar to the left. Trinidad is a staunchly Catholic town, and if you can, visit during services or at Mass (weekdays 8pm, Saturday 4pm, Sunday 9am and 5pm). The music features guitars and maracas as well as an organ, and the Cuban element is very apparent.

Farther up the hill, about 500m (545 yards) behind the Iglesia Parroquial, is the decrepit **Ermita de Nuestra Señora de la Candelaria de la Popa**. Long scheduled for restoration, the main entrance remains bricked up for safety reasons, but the triple spire at the front of this former Spanish military hospital and church has become a symbol of Trinidad. From here, on a clear day, you can see right across town to the blue Caribbean beyond.

Other sights around the Plaza Mayor include the **Museo Romántico**, to the northwest of the Iglesia Parroquial. It was built as the Palacio Brunet in 1740 but the artefacts on display represent the lifestyles of affluent Trinidadians in the 19th century, when sugar was still king. On the southeast side of the square, the mid-18th-century **Museo de Arquitectura** displays examples of different styles of local architecture over the last two centuries. Finally, on the west side of the square, the **Museo de Arqueología Guamuhaya** features a mix of natural history and pre-Columbian Indian artefacts. On the plaza's south side, are two bronze greyhounds.

Santería Traditions

Unusually for this part of Cuba, there's a Santería temple, the **Casa Templo de Santería Yemayá**, just a short distance west of Plaza Mayor at Villena 59. The Santería religion (➤ 16–17) is more closely associated with the Afro-Caribbean tradition, while Trinidad is very old-world Spanish in heritage. Inside the temple, it is sometimes possible to consult Santería priests, have your fortune told and seek blessings from the various orishas (gods).

Iglesia Parroquial de la Santísima from Plaza Mayor

A little farther to the north, and dominating the whole square, stands the tall spire of the former convent of San Francisco de Asís, now the **Museo Nacional de la Lucha Contra Bandidos**, featuring displays of the military campaign against anti-Castro guerrillas in the nearby Sierra del Escambray during the 1960s. There are fine views across both the town and the mountains from the top of the bell tower.

TAKING A BREAK

A wonderful break from exploring on foot is to take an antique steam train ride from Trinidad via the Valle de los Ingenios (► 115–116) to **Hacienda Guachinango**, 3km (2 miles) north of Iznaga, where you can hike or go horse-riding. Delicious traditional lunches are served there.

➕ 180 C3

Museo Romántico
✉ Calle Fernando Hernández Echerri 52 ☎ (419) 4363 🕐 Tue–Sun 9–5 💰 Inexpensive

Museo de Arquitectura
✉ Plaza Mayor ☎ (419) 3208 🕐 Mon–Thu, Sat 9–5 💰 Inexpensive

Museo de Arqueología Guamuhaya
✉ Calle Simón Bolívar 457 ☎ (419) 3420 🕐 Fri–Wed 10–6 💰 Inexpensive

A typical street in Trinidad

Museo Nacional de la Lucha Contra Bandidos
✉ Calle Echerri 59 ☎ (419) 4121 🕐 Tue–Sun 9–5 💰 Inexpensive

TRINIDAD: INSIDE INFO

Top tip Trinidad is unusual in Cuba both for the quality and quantity of the **artwork and local souvenirs** on sale in galleries around the cobbled streets near Plaza Mayor, and private houses sometimes display oil or watercolour paintings as well as charcoal line drawings of Trinidad on their front porches.

3 Camagüey

Camagüey is Cuba's third-largest city; dating from 1515, it is also one of the oldest. Its lovely squares and parks are linked by narrow alleyways and twisting streets, designed historically to protect the city from marauding pirates and raiders. Camagüey, with its range of architectural styles and rich cultural heritage, is a UNESCO World Heritage Site.

Although, unlike Cuba's other major cities, Camagüey is inland and not on the coast, it was still considered liable to pirate raids by its founders in 1528. It was thought that an irregular and unpredictable street plan would confuse and disorientate any such invaders. Still, the English privateer Sir Henry Morgan sacked the town in 1668, and the French pirate François Granmont did the same in 1679. The buccaneers are long since gone, but the road system remains, and it now does an excellent job of trying to confuse and disorientate the unwary visitor. Nonethelesss, there is great pleasure to be derived from wandering along the cobbled streets which link one charming plaza to another, equally as lovely.

Navigating the City

Camagüey is situated on the *Carretera Central* and is encircled by a *circunvalación* (ring-road) that diverts traffic around town. Still, the colonial core can be thick with traffic. Watch out for hustlers who will try to force you the way they want you to go by driving bicycles or motorcycles at an angle in front of your vehicle. Be prepared, ignore them, and if they follow you pay no attention – head for the city's main north–south road, Calle República, which is so narrow that two vehicles can barely pass at the same time. The crossroads where República meets Avenida Agramonte are the nearest thing Camagüey has to a town centre. Turn west here along Agramonte to find a supervised car park at the **Plaza de los Trabajadores**.

The Colonial Core

The Plaza de los Trabajadores is dominated on its east side by the **Iglesia de Nuestra Señora de la Merced**, completed in 1776. The outside, constructed of worn red brick, is massive rather than elegant. The interior is splendid, however, with some fine examples of baroque frescoes and an unusual vaulted

ceiling. There is a convent in the nearby cloister, so make
allowance for the nuns when taking photographs or just
sightseeing. Two blocks northwest of the plaza stands the
neoclassical **Teatro Guerrero**. One block west of the plaza,
the **Museo Casa Natal de Ignacio Agramonte**, is a small but
attractive museum where Ignacio Agramonte, Camagüey's
most famous warrior in the fight for independence from
Spain, was born in 1841. Agramonte led a major attack
against the Spanish forces occupying Camagüey in 1869,
but was killed four years later in another action against the
Spanish colonialists. The house has been beautifully restored
and is well worth a visit.

**Iglesia de
Nuestra
Señora de
la Merced**

Southwest of the plaza, 150m (165 yards) along Calle Cisneros, a small side road leads left (west) for a few yards to the **Casa Natal de Nicolás Guillén** – a modernistic brass plaque marks the place where this famous poet was born in 1902. Guillén founded a school of Afro-Caribbean poetry and was the nation's poet laureate until his death in 1989.

Plaza San Juan de Dios and Iglesia San Juan de Dios

South of the Heart of Town

Farther south, Calle Cisneros leads to **Parque Ignacio Agramonte**, a civic square with a statue of Agramonte, Camagüey's local hero, on horseback. The park is dominated by the **Catedral de Nuestra Señora de la Candelaria** on the south side. Dating from 1530, the church was essentially rebuilt in the 19th century and has been restored. There are two fine stained-glass windows, as well as an unusual statue of a black priest – San Benito di Palermo – inside. Immediately to the west of the church is Camagüey's Casa de la Trova (➤ 123), an atmospheric venue with live music.

Farther south again, about 200m (220 yards) along Paco Recio, the narrow road opens out into **Plaza San Juan de Dios**. This is Camagüey's most distinguished and atmospheric square, lined on the north by some of the city's best antique buidings – look for the *tinajones*, or huge earthenware water-storage jars, which have become a symbol of Camagüey in the garden of a Campana de Toledo restaurant (➤ 120).

The whole of the eastern side of the square – where young children in school uniform are often to be seen exercising – is dominated by the **Hospital de San Juan de Dios**, a former hospital which now functions as the Centro Provincial de Patrimonio, the office in charge of restoring historic Camagüey. This building, with a rather restrained exterior, is notable for its front cloister, dating from the early 18th century.

Following a convoluted path northwest from Plaza San Juan de Dios brings you to **Plaza del Carmen**, the most intimate of Camagüey's cobbled squares. Lined with beautiful 18th-century homes, with a former convent on its north side, its most charming feature is the life-size ceramic figurines of occupants of the street. Besides the excellent restaurants on Plaza San Juan de Dios, the Hotel Colón (➤ 118) is worth a mention. North of Plaza de los Trabajadores on Calle República, this colonial hotel has been beautifully restored and features a stained-glass image of Christopher Columbus above the doorway leading from the main hallway to the open-air patio bar. The bar and restaurant is surrounded by twisting, pastel-painted pillars supporting the balcony.

TAKING A BREAK

Stop for a break at La Campana de Toledo (➤ 120).

🞢 181 F2

Museo Casa Natal de Ignacio Agramonte
✉ Avenida Ignacio Agramonte 459 ☎ (32) 297116 🕐 Tue–Sat 9–5
🖐 Inexpensive

Casa Natal de Nicolás Guillén
✉ Calle Hermano Agüero ☎ (32) 293706 🕐 Mon–Fri 8–4:30
🖐 Inexpensive

Hospital de San Juan de Dios
✉ Plaza San Juan de Dios ☎ (32) 291388 🕐 Tue–Sat 9–5 🖐 Inexpensive

CAMAGÜEY: INSIDE INFO

Top tip During April and May, Camagüey holds the **Festival de Arte Danzario,** an international festival of dance.

Hidden gem A quiet place to relax in the shade away from the main tourist attractions is **Casino Campestre,** a large park ideal for a few moments of reflection, relaxation and watching the locals. It's about 400m (440 yards) due east of Plaza San Juan de Dios. Farther east is Plaza de la Revolución, with a bas-relief monument to Fidel and other revolutionary heroes.

At Your Leisure

4 Castillo de Nuestra Señora de los Ángeles de Jagua

The earliest building in Cienfuegos – built long before the town of Cienfuegos was founded – this venerable Spanish colonial castle dates from 1745. The fort's original purpose was to deny buccaneers access to the sheltered but isolated Bahía de Cienfuegos, and in its time it was one of the strongest Spanish military bastions on the island. It's on the western side of the narrow entrance to Cienfuegos Bay, and can be reached by ferry. Alternatively, take a 20-minute drive from central Cienfuegos to La Milpa and then, from there, a 10-minute boat ride by regular ferry across the narrows. There's a government restaurant specializing in seafood within the castle, but the main attraction is the external view of the Castillo de Jagua itself and the small but picturesque fishing village it dominates.

➕ 180 B3 ✉ 9km (5.6 miles) south of Cienfuegos ⏰ Tue–Sat 9–5, Sun 9–1 💲 Inexpensive 🚢 Ferry from Calle 25 and Avenida 46, Cienfuegos, 8am, 1pm and 5:30pm

5 Jardín Botánico Soledad

These charming but neglected gardens can be visited as an excursion from Cienfuegos, or as part of a drive through the nearby Sierra del Escambray (➤ 159–161) either to or from Trinidad (➤ 106–109). Situated near the Pepito Tey sugar factory, 18km (11 miles) east of Cienfuegos, the gardens were founded by Edward F. Atkins, a US sugar baron who made millions on his estates in Cuba at the beginning of the 20th century. Atkins' original intention was to develop and improve different varieties of sugar cane, but this soon became a passion for collecting rare and unusual botanical specimens from Cuba, the Caribbean and farther afield.

The gardens were taken over by Harvard University in 1920 and administered by it until the 1960s. Tours run from Cienfuegos; otherwise, drive or hire a taxi. Admission includes a brief, though interesting, guided tour taking in just some of the 2,000 species of plants, including many spectacular bamboos and more than 200 varieties of palms.

➕ 180 B4 ✉ 16km (10 miles) east of Cienfuegos ☎ (43) 545115 ⏰ Daily 8–4:30 💲 Moderate

6 Playa Ancón

This beach resort, on the Caribbean coast close to Trinidad (➤ 106–109), is lined by a powder-white beach and is an excellent venue for diving and snorkelling, with good coral reefs not far offshore. If you are not staying in one of the few all-inclusive beach resorts here, you can use the facilities if you purchase a day pass.

The glorious beach of Playa Ancón

It's a good place for a couple of days' sun, sea and sand relaxation on a visit to Trinidad, but not large enough to warrant a one- or two-week holiday. There is tremendous diving offshore, and birdwatchers will find numerous species of water birds, including heron and crane, which inhabit the quiet reaches of **Ensenada de Casilda**, a shallow bay inland of the Península de Ancón.

🞥 180 C3 ✉ 15km (9.3 miles) south of Trinidad

Ensenada de Casilda
✉ 1km (0.6 mile) northeast of Playa Ancón

🔟 Valle de los Ingenios

Once one of the richest sugar regions in Cuba, the Valle de los Ingenios (Valley of the Sugar Mills) is today a remarkably picturesque region, evocative of the Trinidad area's rich, sugar-based past. The valley, east of Trinidad, is dotted with the crumbling ruins of many small sugar mills and estates. Just before reaching the valley, a narrow turn to the left, roughly 6km (3.7 miles)

Torre de Manaca Iznaga, Hacienda Iznaga

from Trinidad, leads to the Mirador de la Loma del Puerto, an attractive viewpoint which offers panoramic views across the valley to the north and east.

The main monument in the valley is at **Hacienda Iznaga**, a once-affluent sugar estate founded in the late 18th century. Dominated by a 45m-high (148-foot) watchtower standing next to the hacienda, the estate is today a major attraction, served by a restored steam train (► 109) that takes visitors from Trinidad to enjoy lunch at the excellent restaurant Manaca Iznaga (► 122) in the restored hacienda. Outside you can view the old sugar mill machinery and bargain for good-quality, locally made lace. Nobody seems to know why the tower was built, but it may have been to keep a watchful eye on the slaves working in the cane fields. It's a tiring climb which is rewarded with fine views.
➕ 180 C3

Hacienda Iznaga
✉ 12km (7.4 miles) east of Trinidad ☎ (419) 7241 🕐 Daily 9–5 💵 Inexpensive

🎱 Santa Clara

Santa Clara, the capital of Villa Clara Province, is a large city by Cuban standards – it has around 300,000 inhabitants – and is a draw for its associations with Che Guevara. The main square, Parque Vidal, is reached by a grid of narrow streets and has been thankfully closed to traffic. The park is distinguished by

a number of fine buildings, notably the slightly dilapidated **Teatro La Caridad** (1885) and the neoclassical **Palacio Provincial** (1910). Next to the theatre, the **Museo de Artes Decorativas** houses a good collection of colonial antiques and paintings.

The main attraction in Santa Clara is the **Monumento Ernesto Che Guevara**, a huge shrine to the revolutionary hero, with his arm in a sling and carrying a rifle. It was erected 2km (1.25 miles) west of the centre of the city in 1987 to mark the 20th anniversary of Guevara's execution in Bolivia, and in 1997 his disinterred remains were reburied here amid much pomp and ceremony. There's an excellent museum of Guevara memorabilia, behind the monument, and revolutionary guards stand about to make sure proper respect is shown – no sitting on the monument steps, for example.
➕ 180 C4

Museo de Artes Decorativas
✉ Luis Estévez y Lorda, Parque Vidal ☎ (422) 205368 🕐 Mon, Wed, Thu 9–6, Fri, Sat 1–6, 7–10, Sun 6–10 💵 Inexpensive

Monumento Ernesto Che Guevara and Museum
✉ Plaza de la Revolución, Avenida de los Desfiles ☎ (422) 205878 🕐 Tue–Sun 9–5 💵 Free

The Monumento Ernesto Che Guevara, in Santa Clara, is the revolutionary's mausoleum

Pregnant Virgin in San Juan Bautista

9 Remedios

Although much smaller than Trinidad, Remedios is the second jewel in the crown of Cuba's rustic medieval heritage. Founded in 1524, it was eclipsed by Santa Clara in the late 17th century and has changed relatively little since that time. The main square, Plaza Martí, is dominated by two churches – the 18th-century Iglesia de Nuestra Señora del Buen Viaje, which has a fine bell tower, and the more important **Parroquial de San Juan Bautista**, dating from 1545. The latter is one of the most beautiful churches in Cuba, notable for its elaborately carved and gilded altar, as well as the only statue of a pregnant Madonna of the Immaculate Conception in Cuba.

At the heart of Plaza Martí is the Kiosko Pando, a bandstand dating from 1909, where live "big band" music is played weekly on Thursday nights. Remedios is also famous for the **Festival of Parrandas**, which takes place on 24 December, during which the locals dance and sing while Remedios' main districts compete for the accolade of the best *carroza,* or float. The highlight, however, is a massive fireworks battle that borders on mayhem.

Remedios is a delightful little town and makes a perfect stopover en route to nearby Cayo Santa María.
✚ 180 C4

Parroquial de San Juan Bautista
✉ Plaza Martí ⏱ Mon–Sat 9–11

10 Morón and Cayo Coco

The medium-sized town of Morón, about 40km (25 miles) north of Ciego de Ávila on the *Carretera Central*, is a gateway to the resorts of nearby Cayo Coco. Morón's only attractions are a large iron cockerel – the symbol of Morón – near the heart of town, as well as a late 19th-century railway station. Then push on across the 27km (17-mile) causeway that carries traffic over the shallow Bahía de Perros to Cayo Coco, one of Cuba's fastest-developing beach destinations. This resort area in the Jardines del Rey Archipelago offers visitors first-class accommodation and beaches.

Another smaller causeway leads to isolated Cayo Guillermo in the west. There's good deep-sea fishing, and an abundance of wildlife, including flocks of flamingoes in the mangrove swamps that surround the south of the islands and along the causeways. However, this glorious world of soft sands is entirely off-limits to Cubans, unless they work here.
✚ 181 E4

The symbol of Morón, a cockerel

Where to...
Stay

Prices

Expect to pay per double room per night:

$ under CUC50 $$ CUC50–150 $$$ over CUC150

CAMAGÜEY

Colón $$

Camagüey's finest hotel, the Colón is really a pleasure to stay in. The main lobby has a wonderful old bar, where the friendly English-speaking bartender serves an elaborate variety of cocktails. As you enter the hotel from the lobby, note the stained-glass visage of Christopher Columbus (Cristóbal Colón in Spanish, hence the hotel's name) over the door. This is followed by a long and stately corridor draped with national flags including those of Britain, the US and France,

overlooking the heart of the old city, there is a period charm to the place, which lends appeal to the somewhat rickety lift. Rooms are clean, service good and friendly, and best of all there's a rather elegant restaurant and rooftop bar offering wonderful views and filling, if rather mediocre, *criollo* cuisine on the top floor. There's a period-style piano bar just off the lobby, but parking can be a problem.

🕂 181 F2 ⊠ Calle Maceo 67, between Agramonte and Gómez ☎ (32) 292314; www.islazul.cu

but not North Korea or China. The hotel has been renovated and updated. There's just one serious drawback – there are no car parking facilities, and the road outside is so narrow that you have no alternative but to drive to the supervised parking area in the Plaza de los Trabajadores and walk back – about 10 minutes – to the hotel.

🕂 181 F2 ⊠ Avenida República 472 ☎ (32) 283368; www.islazul.cu

Gran Hotel $

This is another fine old hotel that has undergone extensive restoration. Five floors high,

pool and email facilities to shops and a taxi service. The decor is classically Iberian and the gardens and pools are beautifully landscaped. Meals tend to be buffet rather than a la carte, and the quality is both fresh and good. This massive hotel is the best of several similar establishments set along the nation's major offshore cay.

🕂 181 F2 ⊠ Playa los Coloradas ☎ (33) 301180; www.solmeliacuba.com

CAYO SANTA MARÍA

Villa Las Brujas $$

In an idyllic setting overlooking the Atlantic Ocean, these beautiful villas are connected by walkways, which run just above the mangroves. There's an average restaurant serving *criollo*, Spanish and international food, as well as a poolside bar for cocktails at sundown. The friendly hotel staff can arrange for various watersports, but most people will be content

CAYO COCO

Meliá Cayo Coco $$$

A very large, well-appointed establishment (under Spanish management), this place definitely aims at the all-in package tour market, but will generally take independent travellers. As you would expect, the hotel has just about everything, from numerous bars, restaurants, a large swimming

to lie back in the comfortable
recliners, iced drink in hand.
☐ 181 D4 ☒ Cayo Las Brujas ☎ (42)
350599; www.gaviota-grupo.com

CIENFUEGOS

Hotel La Unión $$

In a superb location just one block
from Parque Martí, the Hotel La
Unión is very good value. It is far
more appealing than the Hotel
Jagua for its aged charm and its
splendid restaurant, serving some
unusually creative (although not
always successful) dishes. Its
49 rooms surround an atrium
courtyard that doubles as a café and
alfresco lounge. The guest rooms
are well-appointed with modern
conveniences, including telephones
and small refrigerators, although
some of them can be noisy. Hotel
amenities include a swimming pool,
jacuzzi, gym, pharmacy and tour
reservations desk.
☐ 180 B3 ☒ Calle 31 and Avenida 54
☎ (43) 551020; www.hotellaunion-cuba.com

Jagua $$

Originally built in the 1950s by
Cuban dictator Fulgencio Batista's
brother, this hotel has been fully
restored and has enjoyed a recent
refurbishment. It isn't cheap, but
has plenty of amenities, including
a swimming pool, tennis courts,
money exchange facilities, car
rentals, a post office and taxi
stand. There's also a nightly cabaret
by the swimming pool. The
restaurant is a disappointment,
serving the usual bland buffets
and uninspired *cocina criolla*.
Fortunately, there are several other
dining options nearby, including the
Palacio del Valle.
☐ 180 B3 ☒ 1, Calle 37, Punta Gorda
☎ (432) 513021/26; www.gran-caribe.com

REMEDIOS

E Mascotte $$

This beautifully restored colonial
period hotel with charming staff
and a good restaurant overlooks
Remedios' historic Parque Martí.
The rooms are full of character,
with high sloping ceilings,
restored 19th-century bathrooms
– including marble wash basins in
the main bedrooms – and shuttered
windows looking onto the park
or the inner courtyard. Parking is
available for a small charge through
the hotel, but some of the rooms
can be noisy at night. All in all, this
is one of the nicest places to stay in
Cuba. An unexpected gem.
☐ 180 C4 ☒ Parque Martí and Máximo
Gómez ☎ (42) 395497;
www.hotelescubanacan.com

SANTA CLARA

Los Caneyes $$

Just a short distance west of
town on the main ring road, Los
Caneyes is an excellent place to stay.
Accommodation is in "American
Indian" style, comprising thatched,
circular buildings (but with hot
water and satellite TV). There's
a swimming pool, car rental
service, guarded car park, and the
restaurant, which serves buffet
criollo fare, is extensive and good.
The carefully tended gardens feature
Indian-style sculptures and stone
faces set in some tree trunks. This
hotel is very popular with European
holidaymakers and it can get noisy
around the pool and at night.
☐ 180 C4 ☒ Avenida de los Eucaliptos
and Circunvalación de Santa Clara ☎ (422)
218140; www.hotelescubanacan.com

TRINIDAD

Casa Particular Las Palmas $

This lovely *casa particular* offers
simple accommodation with good
food and welcoming hosts. Unlike
a lot of places to stay in Trinidad,
this option is set back from the road
and extremely quiet. However, the
real draw is that it is one of the few
casas particulares in Cuba to have a
swimming pool. Breakfast is basic
but the evening meals tend to be
very good.
☐ 180 C3 ☒ Calle Reale 145
☎ (419) 95200

Where to…
Eat and Drink

Prices
Expect to pay per person for a two-course meal, excluding drinks and service:
$ under CUC10 $$ CUC10-25 $$$ over CUC25

CAMAGÜEY

La Campana de Toledo $$

On the north side of Plaza San Juan de Dios, the city's most historic square, this restaurant has lovely ambience, including a garden setting, complete with traditional giant *tinajones* (water jars), the symbol of Camagüey. The *criollo* food once served here, however, has given way to simple pastas and sandwiches. There's a selection of cold beers. Friendly staff, the quiet, rustic setting and the attractions of the nearby plaza make this an excellent place to have lunch.

🔢 181 F4 🖾 Plaza San Juan de Dios
🕾 (32) 295888 🕘 Daily 11–10

Santa María $$

The restaurant of Hotel Colón (▶ 118) is in the charming inner courtyard, distinguished by elaborate, twisting, pastel-painted columns, with vines growing overhead. The food – *criollo* and international cuisine, with a pretty good wine list – is both tasty and reasonably priced. Although Camagüey is some way inland, the grilled fish is fresh and tender and comes highly recommended. There's a rather genteel atmosphere

---

Brisas Trinidad del Mar $$

This mid-range hotel on the beach boasts helpful, friendly staff, decent food and nightly entertainment. It's an all-inclusive 4-star resort that is particularly suitable for families and couples. Try to get one of the renovated rooms, but all of those on offer are very clean.

🔢 180 C3 🖾 Península Ancón 🕾 (419) 6500; www.hotelescubanacan.com

Iberostar Gran Trinidad $$$

Perhaps Cuba's finest regional hotel, this gorgeous place enjoys a fabulous location overlooking Parque Céspedes and just steps away from Plaza Mayor. Sumptuous in every regard, it is one of the few Cuban hotels to attain international standards. Glittering with marble and polished hardwoods, the lobby lounge opens to a chic bar and restaurant – by far the best dining option in town. There's an internet café and pool table, as well as a cigar lounge. Nor do the bedrooms disappoint, with their state-of-the-

---

art imported fixtures, lush fabrics and contemporary conveniences, including satellite TVs.

🔢 180 C3 🖾 Parque Céspedes, Calle Martí
🕾 (419) 96073; www.iberostar.com

Las Cuevas $$

Just northeast of the heart of town, beyond the ruined Iglesia de Santa Ana, this is a large, government-run establishment with well over 100 rooms in three blocks, plus a swimming pool. It attracts a mixed crowd of foreign visitors and better-off Cubans, but is far below the standards of the Iberostar (and is less centrally located). The standard of food is rarely above average, but at least the hotel has nightly entertainment and a breeze-swept location. The main local attraction, Cueva Ayala (from which the hotel gets its name), is accessible via a nearby stairway. There are exceptional views across Trinidad to the Caribbean.

🔢 180 C3 🖾 1km (0.6 miles) northeast of town at Finca Santa Ana 🕾 (419) 96133

about the place, and the service is friendly and efficient. On the other side of the courtyard, a well-stocked bar serves cocktails.

➕ 181 F4 ☒ Avenida República 472 ☎ (32) 283346 ⓦ Daily 7–9.45, 12–2.30, 7–9.30

CIENFUEGOS

Palacio de Valle $$

The Palacio de Valle is an elaborate palace in Moorish style in the heart of the upmarket southern district of Punta Gorda. The restaurant specializes in seafood, particularly lobster, and there's an excellent rooftop terrace bar with good views across beautiful Cienfuegos Bay. There's a pianist, and in the evenings the staff dress in "oriental" clothing. It's a very stylish place, although, as with many restaurants in Cuba, the tablecloths rarely get washed, and many dishes on the menu aren't always available.

➕ 180 B3 ☒ Calle 37 and 2, Punta Gorda ☎ (43) 551226 ⓦ Daily 10–10

Restaurante 1869 $$

The elegant restaurant of the Hotel Unión (▶ 119) is the best in town and far surpasses the restaurant of the Hotel Jagua (▶ 119). Furnished with period antiques, the mood is gracious and the service is usually efficient and willing. Some of the more unusually creative dishes fail miserably. However, the calamari in tomato sauce and the paella are both tasty and offer value for money. Take a sweater, as, like many Cuban restaurants, the air-conditioning here is usually set to freezing.

➕ 180 B3 ☒ Calle 31 and Avenida 54 ☎ (43) 551020 ⓦ 7–9.45, 12–2.45, 7–9.45

REMEDIOS

Restaurante Las Arcadas $$

There's a good reason for eating at Restaurante Las Arcadas, in the hotel E Mascote (▶ 119): there's nowhere else in town that offers a better meal. The food is *comida criolla* – with the odd Italian dish – but it is reasonably priced, elegantly presented and served in an attractive colonial-era dining room by the side of Parque Martí.

➕ 180 C4 ☒ Parque Martí and Máximo Gómez ☎ (42) 395467 ⓦ Daily 7–10

SANCTI SPÍRITUS

Mesón de la Plaza $$

One of the better regional restaurants in Cuba, this one recreates the atmosphere of a Spanish bodega, with its barrels, bulls' heads, wooden benches, cowhide chairs and shuttered doors. The food is no less inviting and, remarkably, most ingredients for the Spanish regional dishes are usually available. The *garbanzo* (chickpeas with green peas, onions and peppers) is outstanding, and there's sangria and hearty beers to wash it down with.

➕ 180 C3 ☒ Calle Máximo Gómez, Plaza Honorato ☎ (041) 28546 ⓦ Daily 9–8:30

TRINIDAD

Paladar Estela $$

This private restaurant competes against the best that the state can offer. Making the most of its charming garden setting enclosed by high walls festooned with tropical plants, the ambience is delightful. Dishes come well-seasoned and include a delicious braised lamb, while the roast pork is also excellent, and the *mojitos* are strong. The place is almost always full, a sure sign of its quality, but as it seats only 12 people, service is usually prompt.

➕ 180 C3 ☒ Calle Bolívar 557 ☎ (419) 4329 ⓦ Mon–Sat 7–9

Plaza Mayor $$

The *criollo* cuisine is served in an elegant 19th-century colonial period mansion, with attractive indoor and shaded outdoor options. Grilled fish fresh from the Caribbean and served with *arroz blanco* (white rice) is a popular dish,

Casa del Trova / Case de la musica

Where to... Shop

Central Cuba has several large towns, including Cienfuegos, Santa Clara and Camagüey, as well as the beach resorts of Cayo Coco and Playa Ancón. There's also the important historical destination of Trinidad. All have something to offer the visitor in the way of shopping, while Trinidad has the bonus of the best quality art markets beyond Havana and Santiago de Cuba.

SOUVENIRS

The government-run hotel chains maintain the best-stocked general souvenir shops in the central region – often not just the best, but the only ones. In Cienfuegos, Avenida 54 from Parque José Martí to Calle 37, known locally as

El Bulevar, is a well-maintained pedestrian shopping zone with numerous shops selling souvenirs, as well as cigar and rum outlets. The shops are interspersed with small cafés and restaurants.

Shopping in Santa Clara is more restricted as the town attracts relatively few tourists.

Calle Maceo is the main shopping street in Camagüey, with a number of souvenir shops, bookstalls and mini-marts.

ARTS AND CRAFTS

In Cienfuegos, head to **Artex El Topacio**, at Avenida 54 No 3510, for a range of music and books. The **Galería Mayora**, on the southern side of Parque José Martí, displays an excellent selection of local art,

and the salads are more imaginative than the simple plate of cold green beans or sliced cucumber usually offered. However, this restaurant prides itself on its serve-yourself buffet, which is more varied than most buffets in Cuba and definitely worth trying. Musicians are on hand to play *Guantanamera*. Definitely worth a visit.
➕ 180 C3 ☒ Calle Zerquera at Villena ☎ (419) 6470 🕒 Daily 12–10

Restaurante Gourmet $$$

Although aimed clearly at the package holidaymaker, this restaurant in the Iberostar Gran Hotel (▲ 120) does what it does well. Assured dishes are French and *criollo* with a number of international options. The restaurant is open for breakfast, lunch and dinner, but only for fixed menus (no a la carte option). Casual wear is not permitted at dinner.
➕ 180 C3 ☒ Calle Martí ☎ (419) 98070; www.iberostar.com 🕒 Daily 7:30–9:30, 12:30–3, 7–10

VALLE DE LOS INGENIOS

Hacienda Iznaga $$

This restaurant is set in a former sugar hacienda that has been lovingly restored. Outside stands the famous seven-floor tower of Manaca Iznaga, and the valley's old sugar locomotive stops nearby, bringing tourists from Trinidad to sample the fare. This includes cold cuts of ham with cheese, *potaje de frijoles* (bean soup), and a number of specialities, such as pork and sweet pepper stew, *pollo guajiro* ("farmers' chicken"), pork steak "Escambray style" and a good beefsteak (*bistec de res natural*). Unusually, there are also *dulce criollo* (Creole desserts). The restaurant is in pastel shades of blue and yellow, with wooden ceilings and elaborate candelabra. There's a small bar in a separate room to the left. The atmosphere is congenial, and there is an old sugar press at the back.
➕ 180 C3 ☒ Hacienda Manaca Iznaga ☎ (419) 7241 🕒 Daily 9–5

as does **Salón Centro de Arte** opposite it.

In Santa Clara the **Fondo Cubano de Bienes Culturales,** at Calle Luis Estévez Norte 9, sells local handicrafts, while **La Verbena,** at Calle Colón 18, is the best music shop in town.

Camagüey is Cuba's third largest city and this is reflected in the quality of its arts and crafts. **Galería ACAA** on Plaza de los Trabajores sells local handicrafts and paintings. The best music shop in town is **Tienda El Cartel,** at Calle Cisneros 208, off Parque Agramonte. Also good are **Video Center Imágenes,** at Avenida República 282, and **Artex Souvenir,** at Avenida República 381.

The real place to go for Cuban art is the colonial town of Trinidad, where many artisans have set up shop. Paintings, etchings, carvings and Santería (▲ 16–17) religious artefacts are for sale all over town, but especially at the **Arts and Crafts Market,** at Calle Jesús Menéndez by the Casa de la Trova. There's also the **Bazar Trinidad,** at Calle Maceo 451, and the **Fondo Cubano de Bienes Culturales,** at Calle Bolívar 48, just off Plaza Mayor. **El Alfarero Casa Chichi,** at Calle Andres Berro 51, is a great place to buy ceramics made on-site by the Santander family, famous throughout Cuba. Hand-crafted musical instruments are on sale at **Taller de Instrumentales Musicales,** at Menéndez 127.

IMPORTED GOODS

All the provincial capitals of the Central region – and not just Cienfuegos, Santa Clara and Camagüey, but also Sancti Spiritus and Ciego de Ávila – have branches of the hard-currency chain **Tiendas Panamericanas.** These can be invaluable for imported foodstuffs and toiletries. Otherwise, head to the major hotels in the big cities and isolated all-in resorts, such as Cayo Coco and Playa Ancón.

Where to...
Be Entertained

The central Cuban cities of Cienfuegos, Santa Clara and Camagüey are comparatively rich, and support flourishing art and cultural scenes aimed primarily at local people. By contrast, the beach resorts of Cayo Coco and Cayo Santa María target the mass-tourist market and entertainment is restricted to the hotels. Remedios has limited cultural outlets, but Trinidad is bursting with venues for traditional music – anything from Afro-Cuban performances to son.

THE ARTS

The most distinguished theatre in Cienfuegos is **Teatro Tomás Terry** (▲ 103) on Parque José Martí. Musical performances here feature everything from classical to salsa.

At the **Casa de la Cultura,** Calle 37, cultural events are hosted, particularly music and dance.

In Santa Clara, the **Casa de la Cultura,** at Parque Vidal 5, gives concerts and occasional art exhibitions, while **Taberna El Mejunje,** at Calle Marta Abreu 107, provides entertainment Tuesday to Sunday, from traditional *trova* to rap and rock. Saturday nights are given over to gay, lesbian and bisexual parties.

Camagüey is home to the world-class **Camagüey Ballet,** which gives regular performances at the **Teatro Principal,** Calle Padre Valencia 64. Folk musicians play regularly at the **Casa de la Trova Patricio Ballegas,** at Calle Cisneros 171.

Trinidad stages folk music and cabaret performances and

hosts dance lessons nightly at **La Palenque de los Congos Reales**, at Calle Echerri 148. There's also matinee and nightly performances of traditional music at the **Casa de la Trova** on Plaza Mayor.

In Remedios, there are charming live band sessions at the **Kiosko Pando** in the heart of Parque Martí on Friday and Saturday nights.

NIGHTLIFE

In Cienfuegos, **Club Cienfuegos**, at Calle 37, between Avenidas 8 and 12, is a popular drinking spot with both locals and visitors; similarly the Palacio de Valle (▶ 104) offers an unusual mix of Cuban music and a transvestite show.

Two bars in Camagüey are **El Cambio**, at Calles Independencia and Martí, and the **Piano Bar**, at the Gran Hotel (▶ 118).

In Trinidad, visit **Taberna La Canchàchara** (Rubén Martínez, esq Girón), in a 17th-century colonial mansion – try the *canchàchara* cocktail, made from local rum, lemon and honey. In Remedios, try **Taberna Don Juan**, at 12 Calle Balmaceda or **El Louvre**, at 122 Calle Máximo Gómez.

Nightlife at both Playa Ancón and Cayo Coco revolves around the large exclusive hotels, and is generally restricted to tourists.

DISCOS

In Cienfuegos, head to **Club Benny Moré**, at 2907 Avenida 54 (Thu–Sun); alternatively, **La Casa de la Música**, at Calle 35 is an open-air disco for Cubans and tourists.

In Santa Clara, the disco scene is **Carishow**, at Independencia 225. Catering mainly to young Cubans, it's closed Mondays.

Camagüey's main disco is the **Sala de Fiesta Disco Café**, at Calle Independencia 225.

Disco Ayala, in a large cave behind Ermita de la Popa in Trinidad, offers the most dramatic setting of any disco in Cuba.

Larger hotels at beach resorts such as Cayo Coco and Playa Ancón all have discotheques as part of their all-in entertainment, though these are restricted to residents.

MUSIC AND CABARET

In Cienfuegos, the **Centro Cultural El Cubanismo**, at Calle 35, has a full programme of events, including a cabaret on Sundays.

In Trinidad there's a salsa show nightly in the courtyard of the **Casa de la Música**, up the stairway by the Iglesia Parroquial de la Santísima Trinidad. The **Hotel Las Cuevas** (▶ 120) hosts a cabaret most evenings.

In Sancti Spíritus, the **Cabaret Los Laureles** replicates a mini-Tropicana (Fri–Sat) and disco.

There's no formal cabaret show in Camagüey, but every Saturday night is the celebrated *Noche Camagüeyana* or "Night of Camagüey". Locals and visitors celebrate along Avenida República, running south from the railway station. There are stalls selling food and alcohol, and there is often dancing and sometimes a rock concert will be staged.

SPORTS

Facilities for **watersports** exist at both Playa Ancón and Cayo Coco. These include swimming, snorkelling, diving, water-skiing and deep-sea fishing. For details, go to www.cubatravel.cu.

FESTIVALS

In Trinidad, **Fiestas Sanjuaneras** is a carnival that takes place over the last weekend of June. It's characterized by much singing, dancing and alcohol consumption.

In Camagüey, **carnival** is held in the last week of June. The **Jornadas de la Cultura Camagüeyana** celebrates the founding of the city and takes place during the first two weeks of February.

Eastern Cuba

Getting Your Bearings

Eastern Cuba is quite different from the endless sugar fields of central Cuba. There are numerous mountain ranges, such as the Sierra del Cristal near Holguín, the Sierra del Purial south of Baracoa, and the magnificent Sierra Maestra. Then there's the long Caribbean coast, heavily influenced by Cuba's second city, Santiago de Cuba.

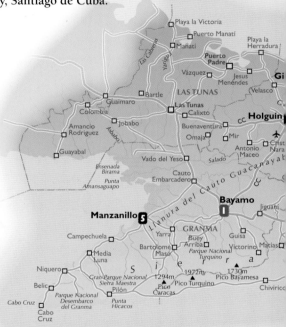

Farther off the beaten track is the isolated and delightful old colonial town of Baracoa, Cuba's oldest European settlement. Dominated by the extraordinary flat-topped mountain El Yunque, and isolated from the rest of the country by mountain ranges, Baracoa is proud of both of its age and distinctive cuisine – the only genuine regional cuisine in Cuba.

Other attractions include Cuba's fourth largest city, Holguín, with its fine late colonial period architecture, and Bayamo – perhaps the most charming provincial capital in Cuba, and revered nationally for its history as a heartland of Cuban independence.

Eastern Cuba – Oriente – is different from the rest of the country. It feels closer to Jamaica and Haiti than to Havana, and it is home to possibly the best musical rhythms, and certainly the most famous carnival in the whole of Cuba.

**Previous page:
El Yunque
rises above
the forest**

**Opposite:
Cathedral at
dusk, Santiago
de Cuba (top);
Sierra Maestra
landscape
(bottom)**

Guardalavaca
8

Punta de Mulas
Cordinez
Banes
Bahía de Banes
Antilla
Bahía de
Nipe Guatemala
Mayarí
Moa
Sagua
de Tánamo
Punta Guarico
9 Conjunto
Histórico Sierra del Cristal
de Birán
Mayarí
Arriba
Parque Nacional
Alejandro
de Humboldt
Bayate
Bernardo
Baracoa 4
Punta
de Fraile
Boca de Yumurí
GUANTÁNAMO
Julio Antonio
Mella
San
Luis
Los
Reynaldos
Jamaica
Manuel Tames
1176m
Pico el Gato
La Máquina
Punta
de Quemado
Santiago
de Cuba
3
Niceto
Pérez
12 Guantánamo
Cajobabo
Bahía
de Ovando
Punta Negra
Caimanera
Imias
Punta
Caleta
10
Gran
Piedra
11 Parque
Nacional de
Baconao Baconao
Mártires
de la Frontera
Castillo de
San Pedro
de la Roca
(del Morro)

0 ———————— 40 km
0 ———————— 20 miles

In Four Days

If you're not quite sure where to begin your travels, this itinerary recommends four practical and enjoyable days out in eastern Cuba, taking in some of the best places to see using the Getting Your Bearings map on the previous page. For more information, see the main entries.

Day 1

Morning
Make an early start in **1 Bayamo** (➤ 130–131) to explore the lovingly restored colonial Plaza del Himno Nacional and Parque Céspedes. After a simple lunch from a snack bar or bakery in town, drive east along the *Carretera Central* to **2 El Cobre** (➤ 132–133), with its magnificent basilica.

Afternoon
Continue your journey to **3 Santiago de Cuba** (➤ 134–137). Arrive in Santiago in the late afternoon, with time to explore the heart of the city.

Evening
Have drinks and dinner on the balcony of Hotel Casa Granda (➤ 148), overlooking Parque Céspedes and Santiago Cathedral.

Day 2

Morning
Explore the major historic streets of old Santiago by foot (➤ 162–165). Have lunch at Restaurant Zunzún (➤ 148).

Afternoon
Drive west along the spectacularly beautiful coast to Chivirico, returning via the eastern ring road in time to reach **10 Castillo de San Pedro del Morro** (➤ 142–143) by 6pm. Watch the ceremonial firing of the cannon (left) across the Bahía de Santiago at sunset.

Evening
Enjoy dinner and wonderful views at El Morro (➤ 148), then head to the Tropicana (➤ 150) for a scintillating cabaret.

Day 3

Morning
Head southeast from Santiago
de Cuba to **Parque Nacional de
Baconao** (➤ 144), stopping at the
Comunidad Artística Verraco (➤ 144)
en route.

Afternoon
Drive to the city of **12 Guantánamo**
(➤ 144) for snacks and fuel.
Continue to Cajobabo along the beautiful shore of the Caribbean, then
snake over the mountains via La Farola to **4 Baracoa** (above; ➤ 138–139),
arriving in the early evening.

Evening
Have dinner and drinks – and maybe a cooling swim – at Hotel El Castillo
(➤ 145). Try the *cocina Baracoa* and watch the sun set behind El Yunque.

Day 4

Morning
Drive northwest along the Atlantic coast through the foothills of the Alturas
de Baracoa to Cueto, then turn south via Loynez Echevarría to visit Fidel
Castro's birthplace at **9 Conjunto Histórico de Birán** (➤ 142). Continue to
6 Holguín (➤ 141) for lunch at the simple Taberna Pancho (➤ 147–148).

Afternoon
In Holguín, wander around its historic plazas before heading north to the
historic port of **7 Gibara** (➤ 141), where Christopher Columbus first made
landfall in Cuba. Alternatively, bypass Holguín and head straight out to the
beach resort of **8 Guardalavaca** (below; ➤ 142).

Evening
Drive out to the Mirador de Mayabe (➤ 147) near Holguín or dine al fresco
at the Atlántico Hotel (➤ 145–146) in Guardalavaca.

⓪ Bayamo

Bayamo, founded in 1513, was one of the original seven towns established by the colonial pioneer Diego de Velázquez. It's probably the most attractive provincial capital in eastern Cuba, at least at its core. With a population of around 130,000, it is both small and relaxed, and long on history – all major elements of its attraction.

The verdant peaks of the **Sierra Maestra** (➤ 166–168) dominate the landscape to the south, while the *Carretera Central* skirts well south of the historic centre, leaving the colonial heart remarkably free of traffic – though you will see plenty of horse-drawn carriages and, at weekends and during festivals, goat-drawn traps for children.

Life in Bayamo revolves around the extensive main square, **Parque Céspedes**. Bayamo was the birthplace of Carlos Manuel de Céspedes (➤ 15), who launched the independence movement and has a special place in the annals of Cuban patriotism. The Cuban national anthem, *La Bayamesa*, was also written here by Perucho Figueredo (1819–70), another famous local citizen, during the anti-colonial wars of the 1860s. Both Céspedes and Figueredo were later captured and executed by the Spanish.

Catedral de Santísima Salvador

Heroes of Independence

Tall, shady trees dominate Parque Céspedes, a spotless square with a granite column pinned by a bronze statue of Céspedes. Nearby, another monument inscribed with the words of *La Bayamesa* bears a bust of Perucho Figueredo. On the park's north side, next to the Hotel Royalton (see below), stands the **Casa Natal de Carlos Manuel de Céspedes**, the national hero's birthplace and now a museum. It's well-preserved and cared for by curators, who clearly feel honoured by their task. Standing next door is the **Museo Provincial**; housing colonial artefacts and the original script of *La Bayamesa*.

On the east side of the square, in front of the **Ayuntamiento** (Town Hall), Céspedes proclaimed Cuba's independence. The first Assembly of the Cuban Republic was here.

Monument to the composer of the Cuban national anthem

A few steps west of the park is **Plaza del Himno Nacional** (National Anthem Square), dominated by the **Catedral de Santísima Salvador**. Dating from 1868 (when Bayamo was rebuilt after a fire), this splendid church features a mural above the altar showing Céspedes blessing the Cuban flag.

TAKING A BREAK

The **Royalton Hotel** is moderately stylish and overlooks Parque Céspedes. It has two bars, one at ground level by the park, providing excellent opportunities to sit, sip and quietly watch the Bayamese go about their daily business. The second, on the roof, gives fine views across the nearby cathedral to the distant peaks of the Sierra Maestra.

✛ 182 B2

Casa Natal de Carlos Manuel de Céspedes
✉ Calle Maceo 57, Parque Céspedes ☎ (23) 423864 🕐 Tue–Sat 9–5, Sun 9–3 💷 Inexpensive

Museo Provincial
✉ Calle Maceo 58, Parque Céspedes ☎ (23) 424125 🕐 Wed–Mon 9–5, Sat–Sun 9–1 💷 Inexpensive

BAYAMO: INSIDE INFO

Top tip In the Plaza del Himno, an old bar called **La Bodega** offers oyster cocktails, a Bayamo delicacy.

Hidden gem Don't miss the **Capilla de la Dolorosa**, a small chapel dedicated to the Virgin Mary on the west side of the Catedral de Santísima Salvador. This is the only part of the original cathedral building to have survived the destruction of 1868, and today it houses the first flag of the Cuban Republic, sewn by Céspedes' wife.

2 El Cobre

The Basilica de Nuestra Señora del Cobre, northwest of Santiago de Cuba on the old *Carretera Central* to Palma Soriano, is the most sacred Catholic religious site in Cuba and the nation's most popular and revered pilgrimage destination. It also has special significance to the Afro-Caribbean religion, Santería (➤ 16–17).

Cobre means "copper" in Spanish – El Cobre was the earliest open-cast copper mine in the Americas, and great piles of slag are visible in the area. However, the real story of El Cobre goes back to 1606, when three fishermen sailing in the Bahía de Nipe, on the Atlantic coast, to the north of Santiago, are said to have recovered a floating Madonna from the waters. The 30cm (11.7in) tall wooden image was of a *mestizo* (mixed race) Virgin Mary carrying the infant Christ in her left arm

The Basilica de Nuestra Señora del Cobre is a sacred pilgrimage site

and holding a golden cross in her right hand. At her feet, in Spanish, was the inscription *Yo soy la Virgen de la Caridad*, or "I am the Virgin of Charity". Legend has it that the image had been floating for 100 years, having been set adrift to protect it from the ill intentions of local idolatrous chieftains.

Cuba's Patron Saint

This miraculous figure was brought to El Cobre, where the first sanctuary was erected in 1608. Ever since **"Cachita"** – as the image is known – was installed at El Cobre, the people of the copper mines seemed to prosper. As her fame grew, so did her popularity, and in 1916 Pope Benedict proclaimed El

Cobre's Virgin of Charity the patron saint of Cuba. The present basilica that houses the virgin was inaugurated on her Saint's Day, 8 September, in 1927. Later, on the same day in 1936, her image was taken to Santiago de Cuba and formally crowned. As though to confirm the sanctification, Pope John Paul II performed a second coronation during his famous visit to Cuba in 1998.

The massive, cream-hued basilica looks most impressive from the approach road. Inside, the arched nave is simple, but there's no mistaking the dedication of the pilgrims who crowd around the tiny figure of the Virgin, dressed in a yellow, gold-encrusted gown and wearing a replica of her crown. The image is housed behind glass on an upper floor behind the main altar, where supplicants kneel seeking blessings, cures, or giving thanks for prayers already answered. (A collection of *milagros* – ex-votos ranging from silver body parts to photographs of loved ones – is displayed at the entrance.)

Tens of thousands of worshippers visit El Cobre every 8 September, Catholic and Santería devotees mingling and mixing both physically and spiritually. It's no coincidence that the Virgin wears yellow – the colour of the Santería orisha Ochún, the sensual Yoruba (West African) goddess of love, rhythm, dance and rivers.

TAKING A BREAK

There are no special restaurants or *miradores* (viewpoints) serving drinks on the winding road between Santiago and El Cobre. Visit the basilica and then head back to Santiago to relax.

➕ 182 C2 ✉ 21km (13 miles) northwest of Santiago de Cuba
☎ (22) 36118 ⏰ Daily 6:30–6 💰 Free

EL COBRE: INSIDE INFO

Top tips Religious mementoes are readily available at numerous souvenir shops throughout the small town.
- Locals will approach you and try to sell small pieces of iron pyrite – **fool's gold** – passing it off as real gold.

3 Santiago de Cuba

Cuba's second city is the country's most important regional centre. An old township established in 1514 by conquistador Diego de Velázquez (➤ 13), it has a rich cultural history and intellectual tradition. It's also the first city of the Cuban Revolution; it was here that Fidel Castro mounted his initial, failed attack on the Moncada Barracks in 1953, and here that he eventually declared the triumph of the revolution in 1959.

Santiago faces the Caribbean geographically and culturally, and is very different from Havana. The roots of its rich culture are founded in the diversity of its inhabitants, a Cuban melting pot comprising Spanish, French and Afro-Caribbean peoples who have lived side-by-side, influencing each other's music, song, dance, literature and art to the extent that the resulting mix has become a distinctively *Santiaguero* whole. There's no other city in Cuba with quite the joyous rhythm of life of Santiago de Cuba, and this is particularly true during the summer when one festival seems to follow another.

The historic Town Hall

Narrow Alleys

Old Santiago is a warren of narrow streets and alleys sloping gently downhill from **Plaza de Marte** westward to the Bahía de Santiago (➤ 162). The most important buildings in this ancient heart of the city are clustered around **Parque Céspedes** and include the fine neoclassical **Ayuntamiento** (Town Hall); the venerable Casa de Velázquez, dating from 1522 and said to be the oldest surviving building in Cuba – it now houses the **Museo de Ambiente Histórico Cubano**, featuring period antiques dating from the 16th to 19th

The twin towers of the cathedral at sunset

centuries, and the Hotel Casa Granda (► 146), with its wonderful first-floor terrace bar. The square is dominated by Santiago's most important building, the **Catedral de Nuestra Señora de la Asunción**, a five-century old church, frequently restored, which dates back to the time of Diego de Velázquez, who is also believed to be entombed somewhere here.

The other significant square in the old quarter is **Plaza de Dolores**, within comfortable walking distance. This is the start of a walk exploring the historic heart of the city (► 162–165).For those who can't make it to the Grand Carnival in July, the simple **Museo del Carnaval** on Calle Heredia in the heart of the old city has displays of carnival dress, floats and related photographs. Try to catch the folkloric dance

show that usually takes place at around 4pm – a highlight of the museum. The **Museo Emilio Bacardí Moreau** on Calle Pío Rosado, just a short stroll away, is Santiago's best museum, as well as Cuba's oldest. It was founded in 1899 by rum millionaire Emilio Bacardí y Moreau and contains many fine examples of Cuban art, from pre-Columbian Indian artefacts, through memorabilia (including weapons, flags and maps) from Cuba's long wars of independence from Spain, to paintings from some of the nation's most distinguished artists.

Moncada Barracks displays its reproduction bullet holes

Northwest of the heart of town is the **Cementerio Santa Ifigenia**, the resting place of many of Santiago's – and Cuba's – bravest heroes. Here you will find the imposing hexagonal mausoleum of the nation's foremost national hero, José Martí (1853–95; ➤ 15); the grave of Tomás Estrada Palma (1835–1908), Cuba's first president; and the tomb of the father of Cuban independence, Carlos Manuel de Céspedes (1819–74; ➤ 15). Many graves in the cemetery are of independence fighters killed in the colonial wars of independence against Spain, while more recent revolutionary heroes, including victims of the Batista dictatorship, are also interred here.

Birthplace of the Revolution

Santiago is a sizeable city, and there's plenty to see beyond the historic heart. About 2km (1.2 miles) east, along the major thoroughfare Paseo de Martí, a small side road, Calle Moncada, leads to the former **Cuartel Moncada** (Moncada Barracks), site of Fidel Castro's first strike against Batista in 1953 and now a school. It contains the **Museo Histórico 26 de Julio**, also known as the Museum of the Revolution. The bullet holes that riddle the walls are not actually the originals, but recreated on Castro's instructions after the event.

West of Moncada, the main highway, Avenida Victoriano Garzón, leads north to Avenida de los Américas and vast **Plaza de la Revolución**. This is the heart of revolutionary Santiago, dominated by the huge **Monumento Maceo**, an equestrian statue of the legendary general who led the independence army against the Spanish colonial presence in Oriente.

Farther Afield

Other museums worth visiting can be found farther out of
town to the east, beyond Parque Ferreiro. This is too far to
walk comfortably, and it's better to take a taxi. Here, on the
small side road Calle 5, off Avenida Manduley, is the **Centro
Cultural Africano Fernando Ortíz**, with a collection of
artefacts from Africa. At Manduley Calle 13, the **Casa de las
Religiones Populares**, a museum devoted to the religion
of Santería (➤ 16–17), has many interesting and unusual
artefacts associated with this Afro-Caribbean religion.

Almost next door – to the north, but also on Calle 13 – is
the **Casa del Caribe**, a small institution founded in 1982 to
study Caribbean life and culture. This organization arranges
the annual Festival of Caribbean Culture, which takes place in
early July, as well as teaching short courses on aspects of Afro-
Cuban music, dance and popular religion.

TAKING A BREAK

Avoid the restaurants on Plaza de Dolores, which serve poor
food, unless you just want a drink. El Barracón (Avenida
Victoriano Garzón, daily 12–12) is a much better option.

➕ 183 D2

**Museo de Ambiente Histórico
Cubano**
➕ 186 A2 ✉ Parque Céspedes
☎ (22) 652652 🕐 Mon–Thu, Sat
9–4:45, Fri 2–4:45, Sun 9–12:45
💵 Inexpensive

Museo del Carnaval
➕ 186 B2 ✉ Calle Heredia 340
☎ (22) 626955 🕐 Tue–Sun 9:30–5
💵 Moderate

Museo Emilio Bacardí Moreau
➕ 186 B2 ✉ Calle Pío Rosado,
just off Aguilera ☎ (22) 628402
🕐 Tue–Sat 9–9, Sun 9–1
💵 Inexpensive

Museo Histórico 26 de Julio
➕ 186 C3 ✉ General Portuondo at

Avenida de los Liberadores ☎ (22)
620157 🕐 Tue–Sat 9:30–5, Sun
9:30–1 💵 Moderate

**Centro Cultural Africano
Fernando Ortíz**
➕ Off map 186 C3 ✉ Avenida
Manduley 106 ☎ (22) 642 487
🕐 Mon–Fri 9–5 💵 Free

**Casa de las Religiones
Populares**
➕ Off map 186 C3 ✉ Calle 13 206
🕐 Mon–Sat 9–6 💵 Inexpensive

Casa del Caribe
➕ Off map 186 C3 ✉ Calle 13 154
☎ (22) 664 2285 🕐 Mon–Fri 9–5
💵 Free

SANTIAGO DE CUBA: INSIDE INFO

Top tips Santiago's most significant festival is the **Festival of Caribbean Culture**
in early July. Throughout this period carnival dance troupes, known as
comparsas, compete with each other and the whole city celebrates with a
non-stop festival of son, salsa, mambo, conga and chá-chá-chá.

■ Cuba's oldest **Bacardi rum factory** (Avenida Peralejo 103, tel: (22) 625575,
Mon–Sat 9–5, Sun 9–1) still produces rum. No tours are given, but you can
visit its well-stocked store and tasting room to sample quality rums.

4 **Baracoa**

Relatively few visitors make it to remote Baracoa near the island's easternmost tip, which is a pity, as this town is one of Cuba's most interesting spots. It is a delightful old town of around 80,000 inhabitants, steeped in history. Founded in 1512 by Diego de Velázquez (➤ 13), it predates both Havana and Santiago de Cuba, making it Cuba's oldest colonial town.

Today, Baracoa isn't nearly as isolated as it once was; until the 1960s, before the completion of the La Farola highway that snakes north over the mountainous Sierra de Purial from the Caribbean at Cajobabo, the only way to visit Baracoa was by sea. It's possible, as the inhabitants will tell you, that this is where Christopher Columbus first made landfall on the island in 1492. His journals describe landing on a headland between two bays on "the most beautiful land man's eyes have ever seen", and he mentions a flat-topped mountain dominating the area. Baracoans agree that this is a reference to **El Yunque** (The Anvil), a massive peak just northeast of town. The people of the small port of Gibara (➤ 141), as well as most historians, would beg to differ, however, and claim that Christopher Columbus first made landfall there.

View across the waterfront

A Town of Fortresses
Baracoa has three historic Spanish forts, all designed to keep English raiders at bay, but none able to do so. Today, the main fort, **El Castillo de Serboruco** (1740), dominates the town and has been converted into an attractive hotel (➤ 145). Of the two other forts, **Fuerte Matachín** (1802) stands at the southern entrance to town by the Bahía de Miel (Bay of Honey) and is now the **Museo Municipal**, while **Fuerte de la Punta** (1803), which once guarded the southern entrance to Baracoa's magnificent harbour, the Bahía de Baracoa, awaits restoration.

The Cathedral
Other attractions include the **Catedral de Nuestra Señora de la Asunción**, which dates from 1833. It's located on the southern side of Parque Central. Outside, in the park facing the church, is the bust of Hatuey (➤ 13), the famous Indian resistance leader, burned by the Spanish at the stake more than 500 years ago.

Inside is the pride and joy of Baracoa – the **Cruz de la Parra**, said to have been raised by Columbus in 1492 and now bound in silver and carefully protected in a glass case. Carbon dating places the cross back to the 15th century, though the wood used is of Cuban and not Spanish origin. It may be necessary to enter the church through a small side door, on the western side of the building, as the main entrance is often barred.

TAKING A BREAK

For a drink or a meal overlooking the Bahía de Miel, try **Hotel La Rusa**, on the seafront. Although the hotel, like much of the Malecón, suffered serious damage from hurricane Ike in 2008, it has undergone restoration. Errol Flynn, Fidel Castro and Che Guevara are all said to have stayed here.

✚ 183 F2

Museo Municipal
✉ Fuerte Matachín, Calle José Martí ☎ (21) 42122 🕐 Daily 8–12, 2–6
🎟 Inexpensive

BARACOA: INSIDE INFO

Top tips Don't miss **Baracoa's regional cuisine**. *La cocina Baracoa* (➤ 41) uses coconut milk, cocoa, annatto seeds, lots of garlic and fresh lime.
■ Artifacts of the region's pre-Columbian Taíno inhabitants can be seen at the **Museo Arqueológico Cueva del Paraíso** (Mon–Fri 8–5, Sat–Sun 8–12, moderate), in a cave in the hills on the south side of town.

At Your Leisure

5 Manzanillo

This run-down fishing port feels a long way from anywhere, but is worth a visit – especially when taking the long drive around the Sierra Maestra (► 166–168). Manzanillo lives chiefly off the sea. The waters of the Golfo de Guacanayabo lap the town's all-but-deserted Malecón and are a prime source of crab, shrimp and lobster; many of Cuba's commercial fishing vessels are based here.

Manzanillo has few visitors, but those who do make the journey are rewarded by the central Parque Céspedes, distinguished by some unexpected and rather lovely Moorish-style architecture. Best is the central *kiosko* (bandstand), along with various other buildings scattered

A statue catches some rays on Manzanillo's Malecón

around the square. The architect may have been inspired by thoughts of Seville, in southern Spain, but clearly wasn't an Arab – the "Arabic script" on the *kiosko* isn't real Arabic at all, but still adds an unexpected Andalusian Islamic element to this remote corner of Cuba.

The Malecón has well-executed reclining figures in stone decorating the seafront in apparently random places, and there are basic rum and beer bars where you can sit and gaze across the azure Caribbean. Nearby, the Plaza de la Revolución has an interesting monument.

✚ 182 B2 ✉ 65km (40 miles) west of Bayamo

6 Holguín

With a population of 320,000, this is Cuba's fourth-largest city and a good place to stop overnight, with a number of hotels and restaurants. Within the city, there are three central colonial squares. To the north is Parque Céspedes, perhaps the most attractive of Holguín's civic squares, with early 19th-century Iglesia de San José at its heart.

Of more interest, just to the south, is Parque Calixto García, with a statue of General García, who liberated Holguín from the Spanish in 1872. The **Museo de Historia Provincial** explains this and other local history. Also known as the "Parrot Cage" because it was once guarded by Spanish troops in green, yellow and red uniforms, its most important exhibit is a pre-Columbian axe-head carved to resemble an Indian head. It's known as the *Hacha de Holguín* (Holguín Axe).

Farther south still is Parque Peralta, dominated by the early 18th-century Catedral de San Isidoro and featuring an attractive *kiosko* (bandstand).

The countryside around Holguín is truly lovely, and the best views of all are from the **Mirador de Mayabe**, 8km (5 miles) southeast of town. There are restaurant and hotel facilities near the *mirador* (➤ 147), known for its beer-drinking donkey.
➕ 182 C3

Museo de Historia Provincial
✉ Calle Frexes 198 ☎ (24) 463-395
🕐 Tue–Sat 9–4, Sun 8–12 💲 Inexpensive

Mirador de Mayabe
➕ 182 C3 🕐 Daily 10–6 💲 Moderate

7 Gibara

This small port is probably the site of Columbus' first landing on the island – despite the protests of outraged Baracoans (➤ 138). It makes a good side trip from Holguín or Guardalavaca, for a seafood meal, a stroll along the Malecón, and a look around Parque Calixto García. Although much of the town was ravaged by hurricane Ike in 2008, it has made a good recovery. The port is notable for its colonial architecture, and the fine views of town and bay from the crumbling fort at El Cuartelón, an old Spanish garrison overlooking the town from the west.
➕ 182 C3 ✉ 35km (21.7 miles) north of Holguín

An attractive terrace of colonial buildings in the port area of Gibara

The turquoise waters of Guardalavaca

8 Guardalavaca

This is another of socialist Cuba's all-inclusive package resorts. There's a long, powdery, white sand beach, warm sea and numerous watersports opportunities, including snorkelling, scuba-diving, deep-sea fishing, windsurfing, sailing and kayaking. An attractive coral reef lies just 250m (275 yards) offshore.

Several adjacent beaches are being developed with all-inclusive resorts. Dolphin shows are held at Acuario Cayo Naranjo, and Cuba's foremost pre-Columbian site is nearby at Chorro de Maita, while the nearby town of Banes has a museum of pre-Columbian culture.

➕ 183 D3 ✉ 54km (33.5 miles) northeast of Holguín

9 Conjunto Histórico de Birán

Fidel Castro's birthplace has been restored and opened to the public. Set amid sugar cane fields at the base of the Sierra de Mayarí, Finca Manacas was the rural estate of Fidel's wealthy father (his mother was the family housemaid and it is likely that the illegitimate child did not grow up in the grand wooden home, as the official guides claim). The village schoolhouse with Fidel's desk front and centre has been relocated to the estate, which also contains the graves of his parents, as well as their Model T Ford car.

➕ 183 D3 ✉ 1km (0.6 miles) north of Birán
☎ (24) 287116 🕐 Tue–Sat 8–4, Sun 8–12
✉ Expensive

10 Castillo de San Pedro del Morro

This is one of the great sights of Oriente – and if you can arrange to be there at sunset it's also one of the most spectacular. This impressive fortress – generally known as El Morro for short – was built by the Spanish in the mid-17th century to

protect the Bahía de Santiago from pirates and, subsequently, from the British. The great bastions and imposing crenellated walls completely dominate the entrance to Santiago's harbour from the east, and are in excellent condition.

A tour of the castle includes visits to the dungeons, bastions and batteries, but the highlight is each evening at sunset, when Cuban soldiers, dressed in the uniform of the independence fighters who liberated the island from Spain, march into the castle with great ceremony. The Cuban flag is raised, a genuine 18th-century cannon is loaded with gunpowder, a coir missile, and discharged across the bay with a powder fuse. A cry of *¡Viva Cuba Libre!* (Long Live Free Cuba) goes up from the soldiers, and the ceremony is over. It's a sight well worth seeing, strongly evocative of former times.

➕ 183 D2 ✉ 10km (6.2 miles) southwest of Santiago de Cuba 🕐 Mon–Fri 9–7:30, Sat, Sun 8–7 ✋ Moderate

Castillo de San Pedro del Morro

⓫ Parque Nacional de Baconao

This is a popular day trip for *Santiagueros*. There's a pleasant beach with a diving platform at Playa Siboney, then the road winds eastwards to the Valle de la Prehistoria, a bizarre theme park devoted to life-size dinosaurs and prehistoric man. There is also a car museum, 2km (1.25 miles) to the east, an aquarium with dolphin shows, and an artists' community called **Comunidad Artística Verraco**. About 10km (6 miles) before El Verraco on the left (north) side, a potholed road leads to the summit of La Gran Piedra, offering great views.

✚ 183 D2

Valle de la Prehistoria at Parque Baconao

Valle de la Prehistoria
✉ 28km (17 miles) southeast of Santiago de Cuba ⏲ Daily 8–4:45 🖐 Moderate

Comunidad Artística Verraco
✚ 183 D2 ✉ 34km (22 miles) southeast of Santiago de Cuba ⏲ Daily 8–7

⓬ Guantánamo

Guantánamo is more famous for its bay, home to the US naval and air base, with its controversial detention camp, than for anything the city has to offer. Check on arrival whether it is possible to view the base from the Cuban military lookout – **Mirador de Malones** – to the east. Direct access to the base, isolated from the rest of Cuba by the largest minefield in the West, is impossible. Guantánamo city is best considered as a refreshment stop on the rewarding drive from Santiago de Cuba to Baracoa. Parque Martí, in the heart of the city, has a few restaurants and a small but attractive church, the Iglesia Parróquial Santa Catalina de Ricci (1862). The **Zoológico de Piedra**, in the hills outside town, is populated with animals carved from rock.

✚ 183 D2

Zoológico de Piedra
✚ 183 E2 ✉ Boquerón, 25km (15 miles) northeast of Guantánamo ⏲ Daily 8–5 🖐 Inexpensive

Mirador de Malones
✉ 27km (16 miles) southeast of Guantánamo City ⏲ Daily 9–5 🖐 Expensive ❓ Check the latest information regarding visits with Gaviota Tours, in Santiago de Cuba

Where to...
Stay

Prices
Expect to pay per double room per night:
$ under CUC50 $$ CUC50–150 $$$ over CUC150

BARACOA

El Castillo $$

This is an exceptionally good hotel by provincial Cuban standards, and would qualify as upmarket anywhere in the Caribbean. Set in Baracoa's largest, highest fortress, El Castillo de Seboruco, the foundations of the hotel date from 1739. There are wonderful views east across the Bahía de Miel, north across the Bahía de Baracoa and Baracoa Harbour, and west to the "table mountain" of Baracoa, El Yunque. Amenities include a swimming pool between the hotel,

open-air bar and air-conditioned restaurant. The latter offers some of the best Baracoan cuisine (▶ 41, 139) in town. Other facilities include a souvenir shop and secure parking on the hilltop outside the fort. It's certainly the best place to stay in Baracoa.
🚩 183 F2 ⊠ Loma del Paraíso, Calixto García ☎ (21) 45165; www.hotelelcastillocuba.com

La Rusa $

La Rusa is a notable hotel on Baracoa's quiet Malecón. The restaurant is excellent; the rooms are clean, albeit simple; and the

prices are reasonable. Yet it's the hotel's history, rather than its location and facilities, which give added appeal. The hotel was established by Magdalena Rovieskuya, a Russian woman whose image hangs in the lobby. According to some, she was a Russian aristocrat who fled the revolution and retired to Baracoa, where she continued to wear a Russian court dress under a burning Cuban sun. Others suggest she simply tired of Stalinist Russia and took the opportunity to move to the tropics. Either way, her legend contributes to the appeal of the hotel La Rusa, not least because she features in Alejo Carpentier's Cuban novel *La Consagración de la Primavera* (The Rite of Spring). Other famous guests who have stayed here are said to include Errol Flynn, Fidel Castro and Ernesto "Che" Guevara.
🚩 183 F2 ⊠ Calle Máximo Gómez 161, Malecón ☎ (21) 42337; www.hotellarusa.com

BAYAMO

Royalton $

Well positioned on the north side of Parque Céspedes, the renovated colonial-style Royalton is top of the range for Bayamo and pleasant, though not unreasonably expensive. There's a relaxing pavement terrace where you can sit, sip and watch the Bayamese go about their business. There's also a rooftop bar with views across the square to the distant but imposing Sierra Maestra.
🚩 182 B2 ⊠ Calle Antonio Maceo 53 ☎ (23) 422290

GUARDALAVACA

Club Amigo Atlántico $$

This large all-inclusive complex catering for everyone from package tourists to independent travellers is set right by the sea. Guests can choose from various types of rooms and villas. Amenities include restaurants, bars, a large swimming pool, car rentals and money exchange. There are children's activites, while for the adults there's a Marlin scuba-diving centre. Trips to Holguín or Gibara (▶ 141) can be arranged by taxi, though the fares are pretty steep by Cuban standards. This is really a place to lie back and relax rather than a base for exploring the surrounding countryside.

🚹 183 D3 ⊠ Playa Guardalavaca
☎ (24) 30180; www.hotelescubanacan.com

La Palma $

This deservedly popular *casa particular*, like so many of these private house hotels in Cuba, is a real home away from home. Large guest rooms with air-conditioning are decorated with pieces created by the owner's artist son. Good food is on offer, both for breakfast and dinner, and the owners will happily advise about things to do in the local area.

🚹 182 C3 ⊠ Maceo 52 ☎ (24) 424683

Mirador de Mayabe $

About 8km (5 miles) southeast of town, this lovely hilltop hotel, run by the competent Islazul chain, offers bungalows recently extensively renovated to international standards, with satellite TV, air-conditioning, telephones and refrigerators. The atmospheric open-air restaurant has stupendous views and hosts a folkloric show. Locals flock to the pool on weekends, when it can get crowded and noisy. A four-bedroom house with kitchen is available and has its own staff.

🚹 182 C3 ⊠ Carretera a Mayabe
☎ (24) 422160; www.islazul.cu

Casa Granda $$

The best hotel in Santiago de Cuba, the Casa Granda has a superb location overlooking Parque Céspedes and the Catedral de Nuestra Señora de la Asunción. Occupying a fine old colonial building, the hotel has been fully renovated and is now under joint Cuban-French management – and this certainly shows in the superior quality of the place and excellent service. The rooms are tastefully furnished in period style and there's a wonderful patio-style lobby bar overlooking the square that serves good meals. For something more upmarket (and more expensive), there's the elegant Restaurante Casa Granda. There are also parking facilities – essential for downtown Santiago, with its narrow streets and pedestrianized squares.

🚹 186 A2 ⊠ Calle Heredia 201, between Lacret and San Félix ☎ (22) 686600

Hotel San Basilio $

A charming hotel in the heart of the city, the San Basilio is long on history. A thoughtful re-modelling of a former colonial mansion has delivered a quality hotel with eight rooms decorated with period reproduction furniture and artefacts. Satellite TV, security boxes and refrigerators are standard, and bathrooms gleam with modern fixtures. A cosy bar is open 24 hours and the small restaurant serves simple meals, but the biggest plus is the location, steps away from the main plaza.

🚹 186 B2 ⊠ Calle San Basilio 403, between Calvario and Carnicería ☎ (22) 651702

Meliá Santiago de Cuba $$$

This modern 15-storey building is architecturally striking. It delivers high standards and the widest array of facilities and services in the city, although it is somewhat lacking in atmosphere. Dining options include the ritzy La Isabelica restaurant, a gym plus spa, shops (including a cigar store and pharmacy), a business centre, plus a full range of tour and car rental options. The huge pool is inviting on hot days, and the city's best nightclub heats up the night.

🚹 183 D2 ⊠ Avenida de las Américas at Calle M ☎ (22) 687070; www.solmelia.com

Where to...
Eat and Drink

Prices

Expect to pay per person for a two-course meal, excluding drinks and service:
$** under CUC10   **$$** CUC10-25   **$$$ over CUC25

BARACOA

Duaba $$

If you're looking for style and comfort in Baracoa, then it's difficult to go wrong with the restaurant at Hotel El Castillo – indeed there are few other even moderately good restaurants in town, so this is both the place to stay and the place to eat. Baracoa is unusual as it's the only town in Cuba with a distinctive regional cuisine (▲ 41, 139). You can dine here on coconut rice and spicy stewed chicken or other local delicacies. The restaurant is air-conditioned and

there's live music most evenings. Afterwards, it's pleasant to have a nightcap in the poolside bar with fine views across the dimly lit town and harbour far below.

➕ 183 F2 ⊠ Loma del Paraíso, Calixto García ☎ (21) 45165 ◉ Daily 7–9, 12–3, 7–10

La Colonial $

A small but elegant private restaurant, La Colonial offers Baracoa cuisine and other *criollo* fare. Portions are generous and the service is good. The house speciality is seafood, especially prawns and lobster, though swordfish is

also generally on the menu. In eastern Cuba, the standard *Moros y Cristianos* (black beans and rice) is often replaced with *congrí*, or rice and red kidney beans. If this doesn't suit you, there's always *papas fritas* (fries) to fall back on.

➕ 183 F2 ⊠ Calle José Martí 123 and Calle Frank País ☎ (21) 45391 ◉ Daily 11–10

BAYAMO

La Sevillana $$

Although this restaurant has dropped its Spanish theme and now offers fairly standard *criollo* fare, it is still the only worthy restaurant in town. If you're staying in Bayamo, or even passing through, this eatery is worth seeking out. The menu includes the usual Cuban staples, plus an excellent *garbanzo* and chicken in red wine. There are two dinner seatings daily, from 6pm to 8pm and 8pm to 10pm. An elegant bar is on hand for post-meal cocktails. Take a sweater for the chilly air-conditioning.

HOLGUÍN

Mirador de Mayabe $$

The hotel at Villa Mirador de Mayabe has a pretty good thatched restaurant serving local Cuban fare and offering really fantastic views across the hills and valleys of Holguín Province. The *mirador* (viewpoint) is the real attraction, but the grilled fish and *papas fritas* are good. Try the local Holguín-brewed Mayabe beer, which is full-bodied but at 3.8 per cent is less alcoholic than Bucanero.

➕ 182 C3 ⊠ Alturas de Mayabe Km 8 ☎ (24) 422160 ◉ Daily 12–3, 6–9

Taberna Pancho $

A good, inexpensive place to eat, this is between Hotel Pernik and Motel El Bosque to the east of town. It caters mainly for locals paying in non-convertible pesos, but tourists are welcome. The food is standard

➕ 182 B2 ⊠ Calle Calixto García 171 ☎ (23) 421462 ◉ Daily 12–2, 6–10

Cuban fare – hamburger, *papas fritas* and draft Mayabe beer, make a good, if simple, meal. If you're in luck, there will be some Tabasco sauce or salsa to perk up the tastes.

➕ **182 C3** ⊠ **Avenida Jorge Dimitrov**
☎ **(24) 481868** 🕑 **Daily 12-4, 6-10**

SANTIAGO DE CUBA

Casa Granda $$$

Perhaps the best place to eat in Santiago outside the Meliá Santiago's own La Isabelica (▲ 146), this is one place you might want to dress up for. The mood is sumptuously elegant, with candlelight by night and liveried waiters; service is a bit stiff, but unusually efficient. The chefs do a reasonably good job with the continental menu, and the place is under French management. The creative seafood dishes are a good bet, and many Cuban staples are on the menu, including *ropa vieja* (beef stew). It's not the cheapest place in town, but here you generally get what you pay for.

➕ **186 A2** ⊠ **Calle Heredia 201, overlooking Parque Céspedes**
☎ **(23) 686600** 🕑 **7-10, 12-3, 7.30-10**

El Cayo $$

This is a wonderful place to go towards sunset. It's on the small island of Cayo Granma in Santiago de Cuba Bay – take a ferry from Ciudamar on the Carretera del Morro – and has fantastic views across the bay towards the impressive medieval castle of El Morro. At sunset, you will clearly hear the evening cannon being fired. The house speciality is seafood, and it doesn't get much better than this. Grilled lobster and prawn paella top the menu.

➕ **183 D2** ⊠ **Cayo Granma** ☎ **(22) 690109**
🕑 **Daily 12-2, 6-9.30**

El Morro $$

A little more upmarket and more expensive than El Cayo (see above), this is perhaps the best restaurant on the outskirts of Santiago de Cuba. Perched on the clifftops just east of El Morro, the restaurant has really good views across the Caribbean. It's decorated in a studiously rustic style and guests can eat inside or on the attractive patio terrace. The menu is a mix of *criollo* fare and international cuisine, with two different varieties of bean soup and baked fish with shrimp and garlic as the recommended house dishes.

➕ **183 D2** ⊠ **Near the entrance to the castle, Carretera del Morro** ☎ **(22) 691576**
🕑 **Daily 12-10**

Paladar Salón Tropical $

Although a little bit out of the way, this *paladar* (▶ 40) is probably the best in town. Its lovely rooftop makes it an atmospheric spot and the service is friendly but not intrusive. While the food may not hold many surprises (as is the case with so many restaurants in Cuba), it is very good *criollo* fare – choose from juicy pork, fresh fish and salad and vegetable dishes. Credit cards are not accepted – as in most *paladares*, and reservations are highly recommended to secure a table at this popular restaurant.

➕ **183 D2** ⊠ **Calles 9 and 10, Reparto Santa Bárbara** ☎ **(22) 641161**
🕑 **Daily 12-10**

Zunzún $$

In this elegant and fairly expensive restaurant, located in the eastern suburbs of Vista Alegre beyond Parque Ferreiro, the cuisine is mixed Cuban-Spanish-international and dishes to look out for include chargrilled lobster, shrimp paella and barbecued chicken. If you're eating *criollo*, then try the tender and nourishing *congri* and – when available – the *yuca con mojo* (cassava cooked in garlic sauce). There's a limited wine list, and the selection of beers should include the local Hatuey brand (5.4 per cent alcohol), brewed in Santiago de Cuba since the 1920s.

➕ **183 D2** ⊠ **Avenida Manduley 159, Reparto Vista Alegre** ☎ **(22) 641528**
🕑 **Daily 12-10**

Where to...
Shop

SOUVENIRS

With the single exception of Santiago de Cuba, Oriente is not particularly rich in souvenir shops. Holguín is a sizeable town but sees few tourists and has little to offer. It's only at the beach resorts of **Guardalavaca** that government-owned hotels run small souvenir shops selling T-shirts and assorted knick-knacks like maracas and Che Guevara badges or berets.

Bayamo is no better, despite its size, but has a pedestrian shopping zone south of Parque Céspedes along **Calle General García**. The city of Guantánamo has almost no tourist traffic.

Santiago de Cuba, however, is another matter. Shops and market stalls throughout the city sell a variety of souvenirs and local handicrafts, aimed mostly at foreign tourists. **La Maison**, at Avenida Manduley 52 in one of the richer eastern suburbs of the city, sells imported and upmarket clothing and perfumes. **Artex**, at the Casa de la Trova, Calle Heredia 208, sells high-quality souvenirs including local Santiaguero music on CD. If you're particularly interested in music, **Fábrica de Instrumentos Musicales Sindo Garay**, at Calle Patricio Lumumba 53, sells guitars, maracas, drums and other instruments. For cigars and rum, head over to the well-stocked **Fábrica de Ron Caney**, at Avenida Peralejo 103, while quality *guayabera* shirts and blouses can be purchased at **El Quitrín**, at Calle Hechevarría 473.

ARTS AND CRAFTS

Santiago de Cuba is an arts hub second in importance only to Havana. The arts scene is notably less Hispanic and more Caribbean. **Galería de Arte de Oriente**, at Calle General Lacret 656 between Calles Heredia and Aguilera, is just one of several galleries in the Heredia area. Another noteworthy outlet is **Galería Santiago**, on the south side of Parque Céspedes.

Galería de Arte Universal, at Calle 1, between Calles M and Terazza, north of the Hotel Las Américas, is a gallery selling paintings. It also puts on various art exhibitions every day except Mondays.

Bayamo has less of an arts scene, but **Fondo de Bienes Culturales**, in Plaza del Himno 20, right in the heart of town, sells local handicrafts and sculptures, while **Galería Provincial**, at Calle General García 174, sells the work of local artists.

Holguín has a **Fondo de Bienes Culturales**, at Calle Frexes 196 by Parque Calixto García. **Galería Holguín**, at Calle Manduley 137, sells local artwork. If you go along to the **Mercado Artesanal**, at 91 Martí on Parque Calixto García, you can watch local painters at work. At Parque Baconao, east of Santiago, the **Comunidad Artística Verraco** (▶ 144) is an artists' community where you can buy at source.

IMPORTED GOODS

All the provincial capitals of the eastern region have branches of the hard-currency chain **Tiendas Panamericanas** (▶ 70). These are just about the only place to stock up on imported foodstuffs or toiletries and pharmaceutical items.

It's also very important to keep an eye on the **fuel gauge** – in Oriente, it can sometimes be 100km (64 miles) or more before the next filling station.

Imported goods are available at **all-inclusive resorts** such as Guardalavaca and Marea del Portillo.

Where to...
Be Entertained

Most of eastern Cuba offers limited artistic and cultural entertainment, but vibrant Santiago de Cuba more than makes up for this, bursting with artistic, musical and cultural energy – not to mention Carnival. Tourist hotels have entertainment.

THE ARTS

Bayamo presents theatrical performances at the **Sala Teatro José Joaquín Palma** in the old church at Calle Céspedes 164; they also give children's shows and musical performances. Cuban folk singing performances are held at the **Casa de la Trova** at the junction of Calles Maceo and Martí.

Holguín's main theatre, the **Teatro Commandante Eddy Suñol** on Parque Calixto García, stages regular top-quality opera and ballet performances. Traditional Cuban folk music can be heard at the **Casa de la Trova** at Calle Maceo 174 (closed on Monday). At the **Casa de la Música** on Libertad, on the corner with Frexes, you can listen to piano and live music – choose from the bar, the salon or the taverna.

Santiago de Cuba's **Teatro Heredia** at the junction of Avenida de las Américas and Avenida de los Desfiles stages everything from classical concerts to rock music. The **Sala de Conciertos Dolores**, at the junction of Calles Aguilera and Mayía Rodríguez, by contrast, is purely classical. Try not to miss the **Casa de la Trova** at Heredia 208, where some big international names perform.

NIGHTLIFE

Bayamo is a quiet town, but visitors should try the **Centro Cultural Los Beatles** (Avenida Juan Clemente Zenea, between avenidas Perucho Figueredo and José A Saco) for Fab Four tribute bands at weekends. **UNEAC** in Holguín, at Calle Libertad 148, hosts interesting cultural events. For something a little less highbrow, visit **Taberna Pancho**, at Avenida Dimitrov, for an enjoyable, old-fashioned, evening of beer and good music.

Nightlife in Santiago is exciting. One of the best spots is **Patio ARTex**, at Heredia 304, for local traditional music. **Club 300**, at Calle Aguilera 302, is popular with both locals and foreign tourists.

DISCOS

There's just one disco in Bayamo – **Disco Bayamesa** in the Hotel Sierra Maestra, 3km (2 miles) southeast of town on the *Carretera Central*.

There are no good discos in Holguín, but dancing is sure to break out at bars or cabarets.

Santiago de Cuba has lots of dance clubs. The classiest is the expensive **Santiago Café**, in the Hotel Meliá Santiago (▶ 146), where a dress code applies. Locals prefer **Sala de Fiestas la Iris**, at Calle Heredia 617, or the rooftop **La Melipona** at Hotel Las Américas (Avenida de Las Américas).

CABARET

In Bayamo, there's only **Cabaret Bayam**, on the *Carretera Central* just opposite the Hotel Sierra Maestra.

Holguín's open-air **Cabaret Nocturno** is 3km (2 miles) west of town on the road to Las Tunas (no performances if it rains).

Santiago de Cuba has **Tropicana Santiago**, at Autopista Nacional Km 1.5 on the *Circunvalación*, and **Cabaret San Pedro del Mar**, 7km (4.5 miles) southeast of town on the *Carretera del Morro*.

Walks and Tours

WESTERN CUBA

Drive

DISTANCE 345km (214 miles)
TIME 2 days
START/END POINT Havana ⊞ 179 E4

This appealing drive takes you through the heart of western Cuba, one of the least visited areas of the country. It's an easy drive, and although it is possible in one long day (with an early start), it makes sense to stay overnight at Viñales rather than heading back to Havana at sunset, especially as the road lighting at night is just about non-existent. You'll learn a lot about tobacco plantations, sample some of the local liquors, pass the time of day with lasso-wielding cowboys and enjoy grand vistas across the Gulf of Mexico. If you make it a three-day journey and stay at Soroa or Las Terrazas you'll also be able to relax in the verdant hill country of the Sierra del Rosario, away from the bustle and traffic fumes of downtown Havana.

1–2

The easiest and fastest way to drive the **Sierra del Rosario** and the north coast of Cuba is to head west along the all-but-deserted *autopista* to Pinar del Río (▶ 78–80). Once you have

managed to find the unmarked entrance road in Havana's Miraflores District, where Primer Anillo and Avenue de la Independencia intersect, it's pretty much plain sailing as far as Pinar, though you should watch out for hitchhikers, goats and cattle.

2–3

A rewarding side excursion from Pinar del Río is the 30km (18.5-mile) round trip to San Juan y Martínez, the small village that dominates the famous tobacco-growing valley of **Vuelta Abajo** (▶ 87). Just before town, turn south to Finca Pinar San Luís, the tobacco

Above: Tobacco and royal palms, Vuelta Abajo
Previous page: A *mogote* in Valle de Viñales

farm of the late Alejandro Robaina, who died in 2010, but whose son continues to grow what is considered to be the finest tobacco in Cuba (40-minute guided tours are offered and there is a small restaurant). The farm is hidden along country lanes; you may need to ask directions.

3–4

Once you've finished exploring Vuelta Abajo, head back to Pinar and then north to **Viñales,** which is among the loveliest regions of Cuba –

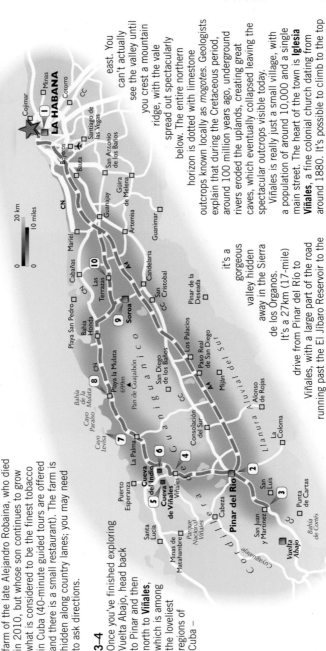

it's a gorgeous valley hidden away in the Sierra de los Órganos. It's a 27km (17-mile) drive from Pinar del Río to Viñales, with a large part of the road running past the El Jíbaro Reservoir to the

east. You can't actually see the valley until you crest a mountain ridge, with the vale spread out spectacularly below. The entire northern horizon is dotted with limestone outcrops known locally as *mogotes*. Geologists explain that during the Cretaceous period, around 100 million years ago, underground rivers eroded the uplands, creating great caves, which eventually collapsed leaving the spectacular outcrops visible today.

Viñales is really just a small village, with a population of around 10,000 and a single main street. The heart of the town is **Iglesia Viñales,** a fine colonial church dating from around 1880. It's possible to climb to the top of the bell tower. From here there are good views of the entire, tobacco-rich valley. Where tobacco isn't planted, luxuriant green foliage and deep, rich red earth provide a spectacular backdrop for the numerous *mogotes*.

There's no reason to stay in Viñales, though several government hotels are located in the area, the best of which is the Hotel Horizontes Los Jazmines. It's a good place to stop for refreshments, however, with restaurants and bars scattered along the main street. The whole village can be explored on foot in half an hour, and there are souvenir and art stalls in the square immediately west of the church. If you're heading back to Havana via the *Circuito Norte* (as this drive suggests), a service station at the east end of the village sells petrol and diesel – remember to top up.

4–5

The real joy of Viñales lies in the area of natural beauty surrounding the village known as the **Monumento Nacional de Viñales**. This comprises a series of conjoined valleys lined by towering, tree-covered *mogotes* and riddled with networks of caves. If you drive north from Viñales along the road to La Palma, you'll pass several of the most interesting cave

complexes. These include – 3km (1.8 miles) from Viñales – **Cueva de Viñales**, a limestone cave that has been converted into a disco at night.

5–6

A farther 3km (1.8 miles) on, the road reaches **Cueva del Indio**, a more authentic series of underground caverns reaching heights of more than 100m (330ft) in places. It can be explored on foot for some of the way, but if you wish to see the entire complex you'll need to rent a motorboat, which takes you across an underground lake.

6–7

Beyond Cueva del Indio, the road swings northeastwards, to connect with the *Circuito Norte* coast road. The road in this area is poor and full of potholes – watch out, too, for *guajiros* (country people) on horseback, goats, chickens, pigs and other farmyard animals, and above all for horse- or ox-drawn carts, which can move extremely slowly. Shortly after the town of **La Palma** the blue waters of the Gulf of Mexico come into sight. About 30km (18.5 miles) farther on, a small road leads off north to the popular dive site of **Cayo Levisa**,

A cavern in the Cueva del Indio complex

yet another small part of the Cuban coastline associated with Ernest Hemingway (▶ 30–31), who fished for red snapper and marlin, as well as watching for German submarines during World War II. The ferry to the island leaves at 10am and 6pm.

7–8

Just 11km (7 miles) farther east, again by the shores of the Gulf of Mexico, is another reminder of Hemingway at the hamlet of **Playa la Mulata**. Here, a plaque informs that "Papa" once used Cayo Paraíso, a tiny island linked to the mainland with a causeway, as a base for his submarine watches from his yacht *El Pilar*.

8–9

After Playa la Mulata, the *Circuito Norte* heads back inland, passing through the small town of **Bahía Honda** and continuing for around another 50km (31 miles) to **Mariel**, a shabby port town on the eastern outskirts of Havana. Unless you're really in a hurry, this route back to the capital should be avoided. Instead, turn right (south) into the heart of the Sierra del Rosario at **San Diego de Núñez** (there are no signs, so ask directions about 4km/2.5 miles east of Bahía Honda). The winding mountain

road leads you up to the delightful hill resort of **Soroa** (▶ 87) with a hotel and restaurant, and spectacular views. Consider taking time out for some gentle hiking and staying the night, and in the morning you can refresh yourself at the local waterfall.

9–10

Alternatively, you may choose to turn left (east) just before Soroa and push on for 11km (7 miles) to the hill resort of **Las Terrazas**, again a fine spot to stay overnight with good food and accommodation. In the morning, there's plenty of time to explore the hiking trails and other sights around both Soroa and Las Terrazas and still be back in Havana by afternoon. Just drive south from Soroa for 7km (4.3 miles), or southeast from Las Terrazas for 8km (5 miles), and you'll be back on the *autopista* to Havana, just over an hour's comfortable drive away.

Reservoir by the resort of Las Terrazas

TAKING A BREAK
Stay overnight at Viñales' La Ermita hotel (▶ 93). Good food is served in the hotel's restaurant.

2 LA HABANA VIEJA
Walk

This classic Havana walk takes you into the heart of Old Havana (➤ 54–56). Visit the city's historic squares and wander along its streets filled with the sound of music and the aroma

DISTANCE 2 km (1.2 miles) **TIME** 1.5 hours
START POINT Plaza Vieja ➕ 185 F3
END POINT Plaza de la Cathedral ➕ 185 F4

of cigars, enjoying the gentle breeze that often sweeps in from the nearby bay. Drink in the history of this living museum and remember that time has stood still here for 50 years, so don't hurry. Take time for a leisurely Cuban coffee, a spot of shopping in the local boutiques, perhaps even pausing for a tarot card reading, before ending with a fine Cuban cocktail at the famous Hemingway bar of the Hotel Florida.

Try to avoid the heat of the day by starting off early in the morning – or ideally late in the afternoon; that way you can enjoy an ice-cold beer along the way and a cocktail at the end.

1–2
Begin at everyone's favourite Havana haunt, the **Plaza Vieja** (Old Square; ➤ 55), site of executions and celebrations. You might want to get a *coco taxi* (the Cuban version of the

Fountain and colonial buildings in Plaza Vieja

Thai *tuk tuk*) to get here from your hotel. Fortify yourself with a coffee or a cold beer in the lovely, local microbrewery, **Taberna de la Muralla** (➤ 68), near the corner with Calle Muralla. Walk to the centre of the plaza, pausing to admire the impressive restoration of the eclectic architecture along with the lovely fountain, perhaps making a visit to the planetarium and cultural centre, **Planetario Habana** (Wed–Sat 10–5, Sun 10–12:30, expensive). Cross the square to its northeastern corner. Take the elevator up the Edificio Gómez Villa to the **Cámara Oscura** (➤ 55) to look over the square – on a clear day you can enjoy sweeping views of the city and peek onto the rooftops of the neighbourhood houses.

2–3
Walk up **Calle Mercaderes** (➤ 55). This cobbled, pedestrianized thoroughfare, whose name means "Merchant's Street", is lined with

5–6

At the end of Oficios is the splendid square of **Plaza de Armas** (➤ 54, 55) which was the centre of government during the colonial period. It is dotted with second-hand book stalls (Wed–Sat) and is the location of the small, green Parque Céspedes with towering palms at its heart.

6–7

From the square, turn left onto the narrow, cobbled, pedestrianized street of **Calle Obispo** (➤ 60). One of old Havana's main arteries, "Bishop's Street", with its museums, art galleries, shops and cafés, buzzes day and night. On the left, on the corner with Mercaderes, is **Hotel Ambos Mundos** (➤ 64), a Hemingway haunt with a small museum and a bar that is open to non-guests, in case you would like to raise a glass

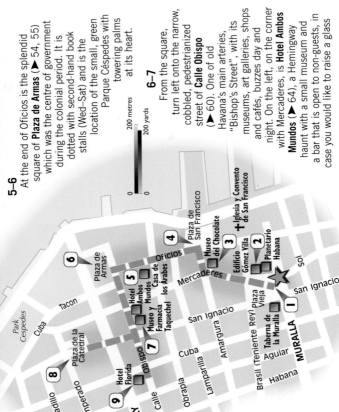

18th-century buildings, many of them housing small shops. Walk past Mesón de la Flota, a restored colonial house that is now a boutique hotel and restaurant. On the corner with Calle Amargura, is the **Museo del Chocolate** (daily 9–8), which is more of a café with memorabilia than a museum, but a lovely spot to go to for a glass of delicious hot (or cold) chocolate.

3–4

Turn right along Calle Amargura to the breezy square of **Plaza de San Francisco** (➤ 55). Facing Havana's harbour, the once a bustling commercial hub, the spacious plaza is dominated by the church and convent of San Francisco de Asís and a large spouting lion fountain. At No. 12 is the charming restaurant, Al Medina (➤ Taking a Break, 158).

4–5

At the northern edge of the square, follow **Calle Oficios**, with its string of colonial buildings. You will pass the small museum dedicated to Arabic and Islamic culture, **Casa de los Árabes** (➤ 56) at No 16, which is worth a visit.

Map labels:

- Park Céspedes
- Tacon
- Cuba
- Plaza de Armas ⑥
- Plaza de la Catedral ⑦
- Obispo
- Tejadillo
- Emperado
- Calle
- O'REILLY
- Hotel Florida ⑨
- ⑧
- Oficios
- Casa de los Árabes
- Hotel Ambos Mundos ⑤
- Museo y Mundos
- Farmacia Taquechel
- Mercaderes
- Museo del Chocolate ③
- Edificio Gómez Villa
- + Iglesia y Convento de San Francisco
- Plaza de San Francisco ④
- Planetario Habana ②
- San Ignacio
- Obrapia
- Lamparilla
- Amargura
- Cuba
- San Ignacio
- Brasil (Teniente Rey)
- Plaza Vieja ①
- Aguilar
- MURALLA
- Taberna de la Muralla
- Habana
- Sol
- 200 metres
- 200 yards

to the literary giant. A little farther on is the quirky, dusty 100-year-old pharmacy museum, **Museo y Farmacia Taquechel** at No 155 (tel: 07 862 9286, daily 9–6, free).

7–8

Walk to the next junction, turning right along Calle San Ignacio to **Plaza de la Catedral** (▶ 59–60), Havana's most important and

beautiful square. Take time to explore the historic baroque cathedral, mansions and houses. This busting square is filled with hawkers, wandering musicians and even fortune tellers, so you can buy a snack and a cold drink, tip a few pesos for some world-class sounds and even find out your future without leaving the square.

8–9

Return down Calle San Ignacio, walking the two blocks back to Obispo and turn right, walking one block to Hotel Florida (▶ 64) on the corner of Calle Cuba. This was just one of the bars in Havana that author Ernest Hemingway was so fond of. He talked affectionately of "my daiquiri in El Floridita, my mojito in La Bodeguita".

Casa del Condes de Casa Bayona in Plaza de la Catedral houses the Museum of Colonial Art

TAKING A BREAK

Al Medina (▶ 66), an Arabic restaurant in a colonial house with a courtyard, is a lovely spot for lunch or dinner.

3

SIERRA DEL ESCAMBRAY

Drive

The Sierra del Escambray is Cuba's second-highest mountain range after the Sierra Maestra in Oriente. Its highest peak, Pico San Juan, near Topes de Collantes, is over 1,100m (3,610 feet).

It's difficult to miss the looming crags of the Sierra del Escambray from almost anywhere in south central Cuba. Strangely serrated, saw-toothed peaks rise close to the coast between the major city of Cienfuegos and the medieval town of Trinidad, dominating the flat sugar lands, which sprawl elsewhere across the landscape. They make a great excursion – one of the best drives in Cuba – and as yet are remarkably untouristed. Be warned, parts of this drive can be challenging (▶ 161).

DISTANCE 87km (54 miles) or 107km (66 miles) including Playa Ancón **TIME** 10 hours
START POINT Cienfuegos ✛ 180 B3
END POINT Trinidad or Playa Ancón ✛ 180 C3

1-2

Leave Cienfuegos by the new ring road towards Jaime González Airport and take the highway towards Cumanayagua. Just 12km (7.5 miles) beyond Caunao, and 2km (1.2 miles) before **Guaos**, watch for a non-signposted road to the left (south) and head south for 3km (1.9 miles) to the secluded Jardín Botánico (Botanical Gardens; ▶ 114), entered by a long road lined with royal palms, near the sugar mill of **Pepito Tey**.

2-3

From the Botanical Gardens, proceed south for 11km (7 miles), passing through the town of Gordo before taking a left (north) turn to the sugar town of **Cumanayagua**.

En route you will pass citrus plantations, especially oranges, as well as more sugar cane than you could have imagined existed. The Sierra del Escambray grows steadily more impressive as you proceed beyond Cumanayagua to **Manicaragua**, the latter more notable for its elaborate Catholic cemetery. The town lies between the soaring mountains to the south and picturesque rolling tobacco country to the north.

3–4

Just beyond Cumanayagua, 3km (1.9 miles) east of the little village of **Barajagua**, a small road leads off south into the hills. This is a one-way excursion to **Hanabanilla**, an enormous, artificial lake high in the hills, that is so beautiful it is hard to believe it is not natural. Here, a hotel of the same name sits. It is possible to arrange fishing trips for trout and bass or just rent a rowing boat.

4–5

From Hanabanilla, backtrack to Barajagua and continue east to **Manicaragua.** This is a small plains town nestling in the northern lea of the mountains – from here, the climb southwards becomes more pronounced.

5–6

At Manicaragua, turn south into the heart of the Sierra del Escambray via the towns of **La Piedra** and **Jibacoa.**
Along the way, you may see converted truck-buses full of Cubans taking a day off to bathe in one of the many waterfalls that cascade down from the surrounding peaks. Looking back from the elevated highway at Jibacoa, there are fine views of the Hanabanilla Reservoir glinting in the sunlight far below.

This is cowboy country, and you will meet more mounted *guajiros* (country people) than vehicles. The road is badly potholed in places but is so quiet as to be almost deserted, and if you stop the car and get out you may be overwhelmed by the powerful scent of *mariposa blanca* (white butterfly), a heavily perfumed white flower that blossoms in the Sierra del Escambray and is the national flower of Cuba.

6–7

From Jibacoa, the road continues for 21km (13 miles) through winding, steep hillside covered with fern-clad trees to the settlement

Landscape around Topes de Collantes

of **Topes de Collantes**. This hill town, billed as a health resort, stands at an altitude of 771m (2,529ft) and is surrounded by lush forests, giant ferns and coffee plantations. It's a very popular day trip for Cubans from nearby Trinidad and for tourists from Playa Ancón. It's also about the only place between Cienfuegous and Trinidad with a half-way decent restaurant, but Trinidad is just 18km (11 miles) away.

TAKING A BREAK
The best place to eat is Restaurante Mi Retiro (daily 10–9, $$), on a hill with valley views, 3km (1.8 miles) south of Topes de Collantes.

7–8
It's a dangerously steep and winding road that leads down out of the Sierra del Escambray

to the town of Trinidad (▶ 106–109), where you may want to stay at least one night. Drive with caution when approaching the hairpin bends, many of which have deep potholes or huge corrugations, with loose gravel adding an extra hazard.

8–9
If you arrive in Trinidad in late afternoon and still have energy for more driving, head east

10km (6 miles) to the Valle de los Ingenios (▶ 115–116) to explore the old sugar estates and enjoy views over the valley from the tower at Manaca Iznaga (▶ 116). Return to Trinidad for the sunset or, better yet, from Trinidad drive south 15km (9 miles) to the beach resort at Playa Ancón (▶ 114–115) and enjoy a cold beer watching the sun set over the Caribbean.

Panoramic view of Playa Ancón at sunset

SANTIAGO DE CUBA
4
Walk

DISTANCE 2.5km (1.5 miles) one way **TIME** 3 hours
START POINT Iglesia Nuestra Señora de Dolores, Plaza de Dolores ✚ 186 C3
END POINT Museo de la Lucha Clandestina ✚ 186 A2

This walk takes you through the historic heart of Santiago de Cuba (▶ 134–137), Cuba's second-largest city and one of the nation's most historic and vibrant cultural hubs. The walk starts in the eastern part of the city centre at Plaza de Dolores and takes you westwards through the central part of the Old City past the Catedral de Nuestra Señora de la Asunción towards the Caribbean. This is best viewed from the *mirador* (viewpoint) of the Balcón de Velázquez, which you reach towards the end of the walk.

The elegant and well-shaded Plaza de Dolores makes a convenient starting point for an exploration of old Santiago de Cuba, not least because several restaurants cluster around the square and it's easy to stop for a cup of coffee or eat breakfast to refuel before setting off on the walk.

Santiago's Catedral de Nuestra Señora de la Asunción dates from 1528

1–2
At the western end of Plaza de Dolores, just off Calle Aguilera on the southern side of the street, stands the **Sala de Conciertos Dolores**, housed in the former church of Iglesia Nuestra Señora de Dolores. Once a building of some note, it was badly damaged by fire in the 1970s and rebuilt as a concert hall. It's a good place to watch young students of music practising under the tutelage of their professors, with some saxophone and guitar players actually sitting in the shade on the raised steps going through their routines.

2–3
Immediately to the west of the church is the lovely Plaza de Dolores (▶ 135). This shaded square is cool at almost all times of the day, and is a popular place for Cubans, especially musicians, to hang out. There are usually plenty of interesting characters around, and not just hustlers – people anxious

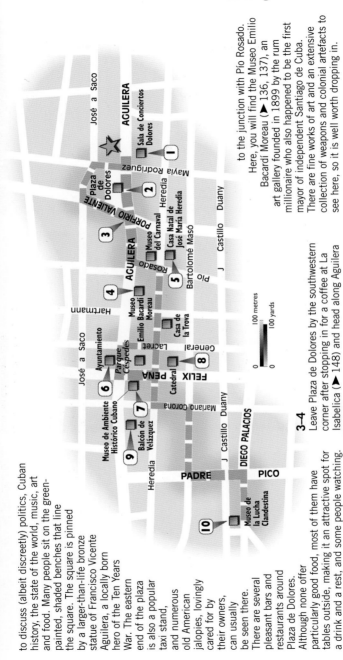

to discuss (albeit discreetly) politics, Cuban history, the state of the world, music, art and food. Many people sit on the green-painted, shaded benches that line the square. The square is pinned by a larger-than-life bronze statue of Francisco Vicente Aguilera, a locally born hero of the Ten Years War. The eastern end of the plaza is also a popular taxi stand, and numerous old American jalopies, lovingly cared for by their owners, can usually be seen there. There are several pleasant bars and restaurants around Plaza de Dolores. Although none offer particularly good food, most of them have tables outside, making it an attractive spot for a drink and a rest, and some people watching.

3–4

Leave Plaza de Dolores by the southwestern corner after stopping in for a coffee at La Isabelica (▶ 148) and head along Aguilera to the junction with Pío Rosado. Here, you will find the Museo Emilio Bacardí Moreau (▶ 136, 137), an art gallery founded in 1899 by the rum millionaire who also happened to be the first mayor of independent Santiago de Cuba. There are fine works of art and an extensive collection of weapons and colonial artefacts to see here, so it is well worth dropping in.

4–5

A short walk south along Pío Rosado brings you to **Calle Heredia**, a narrow, picturesque street with two small museums, each worth a visit. The first is the small Museo del Carnaval (▲ 135–136), which provides some idea of the wild times occurring each July, but of course is no substitute for the real thing. Diagonally opposite is the **Casa Natal de José María Heredia**, a Cuban poet and nationalist born here in 1803. Heredia was driven into exile by the Spanish authorities because of his nationalist views and died in Mexico in 1839.

5–6

Calle Heredia is a particularly musical street, even by Cuban standards, and Latin-Caribbean rhythms generally emanate from the nearby Casa de la Trova (▲ 150), just by the southeastern entrance to Parque Céspedes (▲ 134), the city's most important square. Parque Céspedes, named after the country's first independence leader (▲ 15), is really the heart of historic Santiago de Cuba. Immediately to the right on entering the park is the classy Hotel Casa Granda (▲ 146), an excellent place to stop for refreshments and to watch the goings-on in the busy square from

the large, shaded first-floor bar and restaurant. At the heart of the leafy square is a bust of **Carlos Manuel de Céspedes**. To the north of the square is the very fine **Ayuntamiento** or Town Hall, which is unfortunately closed to visitors. Fidel Castro gave his victory speech from the balcony on 1 January 1959, announcing that Batista had fled the country.

6–7

To the northwest of the square is the **Museo de Ambiente Histórico Cubano**, a beautifully restored colonial building also known as the Casa de Velázquez (▲ 134–135, 137). Said to be the oldest surviving house in Cuba, it now displays various paintings and antiques from the colonial period. The first floor was once a trading house, while upstairs was the personal residence of conquistador Diego de Velázquez (▲ 13).

7–8

Dominating the square from its south side is the magnificent Catedral de Nuestra Señora de la Asunción (▲ 135). Originally constructed in 1528, it underwent considerable restoration four centuries later and is still a splendid edifice. The remains of the famed Diego de

Casa de la Trova, the place to hear Cuban folk music

The stairs ascending from Padre Pico

Velásquez are said to be interred here, though nobody seems quite sure where. The building has five naves supporting a beautifully coffered ceiling and dome. Unfortunately, it's often closed except during services, but the small **Museo Arquidiocesano** (inexpensive) on the south side of the cathedral houses religious artefacts, furniture and paintings and is open Monday to Saturday 9:30 to 5:30.

8–9

Leave Parque Céspedes by walking west one block on Calle Heredia and walk south one block along Calle Mariano Corona. On the right (west) of the road, atop an old Spanish fort, is the **Balcón de Velázquez** lookout point, where you can sip a cold drink while taking in the magnificent views across Santiago Harbour.

9–10

Turn right and continue one block. Turn left onto Padre Pico and ascend the flight of steps known as the **Padre Pico** stairs. From here, it's a short walk west up the **Museo de la Lucha Clandestina** (Museum of the Clandestine Struggle) at No 1 (Tue–Sun

9–5, inexpensive). Exhibits document the struggle against the Batista dictatorship. The house at Calle General Jesús Rabí 6 is Fidel Castro's lodgings while he was a student in Santiago de Cuba (not open to the public). From here, take a taxi to Plaza de Dolores.

TAKING A BREAK
A good place to lunch is the lobby bar overlooking Parque Céspedes at the Casa Granda hotel (▶ 146).

5 SIERRA MAESTRA

Drive

This is undoubtedly one of the most spectacular drives in Cuba, and well worth the effort. It is a long way, but can be halved if time is tight by starting in Marea del Portillo instead of Bayamo. Otherwise, and ideally, make it a relaxing and invigorating two-day drive taking in some of the most breathtaking scenery in eastern Cuba lying between Bayamo and Santiago de Cuba, two of Oriente's most interesting cities.

DISTANCE 215km (133 miles) or 160km (99 miles) **TIME** 2 days
START POINT Bayamo or Marea del Portillo ✚ 182 B2
END POINT Santiago de Cuba ✚ 183 D2

1–2

Bayamo (▶ 130–131) is a historically important town with much to see and a great place to overnight. From here, starting as early as possible, head out to the southwest of the city along the narrow but well-maintained road to **Barranca**. This is cattle country, and the sugar cane fields of central Cuba are increasingly replaced by open grazing country. From Barranca, continue west through **Veguitas** to Yara, 46km (28.5 miles) west of Bayamo. **Yara** has great importance in

Cuba's history of nationalism. It was here that Carlos Manuel de Céspedes (▶ 15), after freeing his slaves, fought his first battle against the Spanish in October 1868. The town is famous for Céspedes' *Grito de Yara* or "Yara Declaration", in which he declared Cuba's independence. These events are commemorated at the **Museo Municipal** (Tue–Sun 9–12, 1:30–5:30, inexpensive).

2–3

Just 40km (25 miles) south of Yara, passing through the small cattle town of Bartolomé Masó, is the **Gran Parque Nacional Sierra Maestra**, the highest mountain range in the country and famous as Fidel Castro's main redoubt in his struggle to overthrow the dictator Fulgencio Batista (▶ 15). Driving

into the park involves climbing steep concrete access roads with strange, narrow side-tracks – these latter are used by the locals as a rapid form of transport aboard wheeled trolleys.

Bahía de Santiago de Cuba

The scenery as you climb towards Santo Domingo is spectacular, but the corrugated roads are very steep in places and pretty tough on any vehicle, so it's not for every driver. There's a fine viewpoint at **Balcón de la Sierra**, immediately above the Paso Malo Reservoir, then the road winds into the hills beyond **Providencia** to its destination at **Santo Domingo**.

This is as far as the drive into the Sierra Maestra goes. It's possible to trek much farther, all the way to the summit of **Pico Turquino**, at 1,972m (6,468ft) the highest mountain in the country, surrounded by the national park of the same name. However, special permits are required (obtainable at the Park Office in Santo Domingo), and you need to be really fit. The trekking fee includes a mandatory guide, who can if you wish take you to visit Castro's guerrilla headquarters at **La Comandancia de la Plata.**

3–4

Many people will prefer to turn round at Santo Domingo and retrace their route to Yara. From here, it's a straightforward 23km (14-mile) drive across more cattle and sugar country to the port of Manzanillo (▶ 140). This isolated fishing port is a good place to take

a break, especially at one of the bars along the Malecón or seafront. The real attraction, however, is **Parque Céspedes**, Manzanillo's central square, with its Andalusian-style Moorish architecture. The best example of this art form is the central *kiosko* (bandstand).

4–5

Continue southwest by the shores of the Caribbean past the **Museo Histórico de la Demajagua** (Mon–Sat 8–12, 1–5, Sun 8–1, inexpensive), 10km (6 miles) south of town, formerly the family estate of Carlos Manuel de

Céspedes, where the great patriot rang the bell freeing his slaves in 1868. It remains a place of nationalist pride and pilgrimage.

5–6

The road continues southwest through Media Luna, birthplace of Celia Sánchez, "first lady" of the Cuban Revolution, before swinging inland after 12km (7.5 miles) to Pilón. From this point to Santiago de Cuba, the highway hugs the Caribbean. This area is arid, with cacti and scrub predominant. Just east of Pilón at **Punta de Piedra**, there's a reasonable hotel at **Punta de Piedra**, Villa Punta de Piedra (tel: 59 7062, $$), facing the turquoise Caribbean, which makes a good place to stop for a meal. If, on the other hand, you're intending an overnight stop, drive the farther 7km (4.3 miles) to **Marea del Portillo**, where several modest resort hotels provide decent accommodation although the food in all the restaurants is mediocre. If you visited Santo Domingo, you will most probably need to overnight here before continuing east.

6–7

From Marea del Portillo, the drive to **Santiago del Cuba** is pure pleasure. There's hardly any

Turquino National Park and Pico Turquino

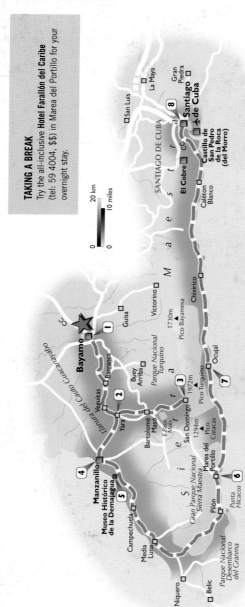

traffic and the magnificent Sierra Maestra rises sheer to your north, while the Caribbean laps or lashes at the southern side of the highway, sometimes so close that you're almost in the waves. You should watch for landslips and stray boulders. As usual in

Cuba, there are no lights at all at night. You won't see anything but buzzards, goat-herds and cowboys for the remainder of the three-hour drive to Santiago – though if you're lucky, near Ocujal, the clouds will part to reveal the towering peak of **Pico Turquino** (▶ 167).

7–8

Beyond Pico Turquino, the coast road takes you through wild country, passing the small towns of Chivirico and Caletón Blanco before skirting **Bahía de Santiago de Cuba** to enter Santiago de Cuba via its southwestern suburbs.

Practicalities

BEFORE YOU GO

WHAT YOU NEED

		UK	Germany	USA	Canada	Australia	Ireland	Netherlands	Spain
● Required ○ Suggested ▲ Not required △ Not applicable	Some countries require a passport to remain valid for a minimum period (usually at least six months) beyond the date of entry – contact your consulate or embassy or a travel agent for details.								
Passport (also check visa requirements)		●	●	●	●	●	●	●	●
Tourist Card (for all holiday travel*)		●	●	●	●	●	●	●	●
Onward or Return Ticket		●	●	●	●	●	●	●	●
Health Inoculations (check with your doctor before travel)		▲	▲	▲	▲	▲	▲	▲	▲
Health Documentation (► 174, Health)		△	△	△	△	△	△	△	△
Health and Travel Insurance		●	●	●	●	●	●	●	●
Driving Licence (international) for car rental		●	●	●	●	●	●	●	●

*Purchase in advance from the Cuban Embassy or tour operator in your home country. Valid for up to 30 days, or 90 days for Canadians; can be extended in Havana.

WHEN TO GO

Havana

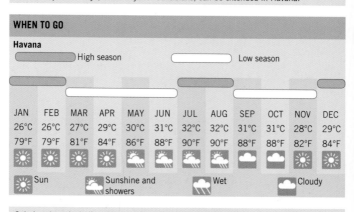

	JAN	FEB	MAR	APR	MAY	JUN	JUL	AUG	SEP	OCT	NOV	DEC
	26°C	26°C	27°C	29°C	30°C	31°C	32°C	32°C	31°C	31°C	28°C	29°C
	79°F	79°F	81°F	84°F	86°F	88°F	90°F	90°F	88°F	88°F	82°F	84°F

High season / Low season

Sun · Sunshine and showers · Wet · Cloudy

Cuba's subtropical climate has only two seasons, the **rainy summer** (May to October) and the relatively **dry winter** (November to April). January to April is the **sunniest time to visit**, while the **hurricane season** generally runs from June to November. Hurricanes are more frequent in the west of the island, particularly in Pinar del Río and Havana provinces. Rainstorms tend to be short but heavy, and affect the central cordillera more than the coast. The heaviest rains are generally in September and October. Rainfall tends to be heavier in the east of the island. Because of the island's long, thin shape, few places are far from the sea and there is generally a **cooling sea breeze**. In winter, it can be chilly in the higher mountains, but it's never really cold. **Humidity** ranges from the high 70s in winter to the low 80s in summer – enough to make breeze and shade attractive.

GETTING ADVANCE INFORMATION

Websites
- www.cubagob.cu
- www.cubatravel.cu
- www.habaguanexhotels.com
- www.lahabana.com
- http://havanajournal.com

In the UK
Cuba Tourist Board
154 Shaftesbury Avenue,
London WC2H 8HL
☎ 020 7240 6655;
www.travel2cuba.co.uk

In the US
There is no official Cuban tourist representation in the US.

GETTING THERE

By Air Scheduled and charter flights operate from Britain, Continental Europe, Canada, Mexico, Jamaica and numerous other Latin American and Caribbean countries. Licensed charter flights operate from the US (notably Miami) but **only** for those legally permitted to travel to Cuba and to spend money there – generally Cuban exiles. Major carriers serving Cuba include **Air Canada** (www.aircanada.com), **Air France** (www.airfrance.com), **Air Europe** (www.aireurope.it), **Cubana** (www.cubana.cu), **Virgin Atlantic** (www.virginatlantic.com), **Iberia** (www.iberia.com) and the Netherlands-based **Martinair** (www.martinair.com).

Most independent travellers fly into Havana's José Martí International Airport, but package tourists on all-inclusive trips may often fly to regional airports, such as Cayo Coco, Cienfuegos, Santiago de Cuba and Varadero. In the latter case, all local travel arrangements will have been made in advance by the responsible travel agency. There are no direct scheduled flights between the US and Cuba.

By Sea There are **no scheduled ferry services** from nearby countries to Cuba, although some cruise liners do call at the island. Access by private yacht or cruiser is both permitted and relatively easy but be sure to contact the port authorities first, before you arrive in Cuban waters.

TIME

Cuban local time is the same as Eastern Standard Time in the US, which is five hours behind Greenwich Mean Time (GMT -5). Clocks are turned forwards an hour in late March/early April and back an hour in early October.

CURRENCY AND FOREIGN EXCHANGE

There are two currencies in Cuba. Cubans are paid in **pesos** (worth 100 centavos), which have an exchange rate of 26:1 with the US dollar. However, there is virtually nothing of value to buy using pesos, except street food and goods in farmers markets. Tourists must use **convertible pesos (CUC)** for all transactions. There are official bureaux de change called *cadeca* (found in cities throughout Cuba), which change foreign currency for convertible pesos. Convertible pesos can only be converted in Cuba and will be useless if you take them home.

US dollars are no longer accepted for direct payment, and a 10 per cent surcharge applies for exchanging dollars for convertible pesos. Euros are accepted in hotels and restaurants in Varadero, Cayo Coco and Cayo Largo. Cash and travellers' cheques in euros, Canadian dollars or US dollars can be exchanged at banks and major hotels, though travellers' cheques issued by US banks may be refused.

ATMs are increasingly available in Cuba, in the main cities and tourist areas, but cards issued in the US will not be accepted.

Credit cards are generally accepted only at major hotels and tourist destinations, and even then the connection may not be working. Credit cards issued or processed by US institutions are unusable in Cuba.

In Canada
Cuban Tourist Board
1200 Bay Street
No 305, Toronto
Ontario M5R 2A5
☎ 0416 362 0700;
www.gocuba.ca

In Spain
Officina de Promoción e
Información Turística de Cuba
Paseo de la Habana 54
Madrid 28036
☎ 34 91 411 3097

In France
Office de Tourisme de Cuba
280 Boulevard Raspail
75014 Paris
☎ 33 1 4538 9010;
www.cubatourisme.fr

WHEN YOU ARE THERE

NATIONAL HOLIDAYS

1 Jan	Liberation Day (in 1959)
1 May	International Labour Day
26 Jul	National Rebellion Day (Assault on the Moncada Barracks in 1953)
10 Oct	Start of First War of Independence (1868)
25 Dec	Christmas Day

There are unofficial holidays on 31 December, 25 and 27 July. On many other significant days, such as the birthday of José Martí (28 January) and the Bay of Pigs Victory (19 April), shops and offices may close.

ELECTRICITY

 Cuba operates on a 110-volt AC (60 cycles) system nationwide. Brownouts and power shortages are common. Most outlets use US-style flat, two- or three-pin plugs. Some use 220-volt AC.

OPENING HOURS

○ Shops
● Offices
● Banks
● Post Offices
● Museums/Monuments
● Pharmacies

8am 9am 10am noon 1pm 2pm 4pm 5pm 7pm

☐ Day   ☐ Midday   ☐ Evening

Shops Opening times are flexible, depending on availability of stock. Late-evening shopping is rare.

Churches Services are held on Sunday morning and evening, otherwise many churches remain locked.

Museums Opening and closing times vary. Last entry is 30 minutes before closing.

TIPS/GRATUITIES

Always try to tip in Cuba, even if a service charge is included, as workers struggle to survive on less than a dollar a day. The following rates are suggested:

Restaurants	5–10%
Bars	Leave change
Taxis	Leave change
Porters	CUC5
Chambermaids	CUC2/day
Musicians (restaurants)	CUC2–5

FREEDOM TO TRAVEL

Restrictions on travel to Cuba for Americans are gradually being lifted under the Obama administration. Cuban expats living in Miami can visit relatives in Cuba and, since 2011, US citizens have been allowed to travel to the island as part of religious or educational visits.

TIME DIFFERENCES

GMT	**Cuba**	**US East**	**Germany**	**Spain**	**Australia**
12 noon	7am	7am	1pm	1pm	Sydney 10pm

STAYING IN TOUCH

The postal system in Cuba is slow but usually reliable – allow six weeks for North America and perhaps longer for Europe. All towns have at least one post office, some several. Many gift stores and hotels sell postage-prepaid envelopes and postcards.

Cuba's phone system is generally slow and antiquated. Phone cards can be bought at most major tourist hotels and some other outlets, and can be used to dial abroad. Internal telephone numbers change frequently, and numbers throughout Cuba are gradually being changed to seven digits as new digital exchanges are installed. It's much cheaper to call abroad from a public call box using a phone card than from your hotel bedroom.

International Dialing Codes

UK:	44
US/Canada:	1
Germany:	49
Spain:	34
Netherlands:	31
Australia:	61

Mobile phones Costs of calls from mobile phones are prohibitively expensive for most locals. Some foreign phones work in Cuba, but check with your provider. It is possible to rent a mobile phone on arrival, from Cubacel (www.cubacel.cu) with a local SIM card.

WiFi and Internet Connections in Cuba are painfully slow with access to Cubans severely restricted, although this aspect of daily life in the country is improving slowly. Internet access is mostly only found in upmarket tourist hotels and prices are relatively expensive, with poor connection speed. Internet booths are being opened by the Cuban telecommunications company ETECSA and WiFi spots are appearing.

PERSONAL SAFETY

- Cuba is probably the safest destination in Latin America, but in large cities and at night you should still be careful of pick-pockets and bag-snatchers.
- Theft of rental cars (or parts of rental cars) is also on the rise. Never leave valuables in your car.
- Personal violence against tourists is most unusual outside major cities, but is not unknown in city slum districts.
- Women may be subject to the attentions of ultra-macho males. Avoiding direct eye contact and ignoring them is usually the best policy.
- Hustlers (*jineteros*) and prostitutes (*jineteras*) are an increasing problem (► 35). Ignoring them is usually the best policy.
- Don't exchange money on the streets: you will probably receive counterfeit notes. Try to avoid receiving CUC50 notes as many counterfeit notes are in operation.

POLICE	**116**
FIRE	**115**
AMBULANCE	**118**

HEALTH

 Insurance Medical insurance is strongly recommended, though treatment costs are low in comparison to the US. Resorts and major cities have clinics for tourists. Health services are relatively good in tourist zones, but medicines are rarely available elsewhere and X-ray and other machines are often broken.

 Dental services Dental care should be covered by your medical insurance. Check that it is, as you will be required to pay for any treatment. Standards of dental care in Cuba are poor, so be sure to have a check-up with your own dentist before you leave for Cuba.

 Weather The Caribbean sun can be extremely strong, so it's best to avoid exposure to it between 10am and 3pm. You can still enjoy the sun in the morning and evening hours, but use a high-factor sunscreen liberally, and also wear a hat and sunglasses.

 Drugs Pharmacies in Cuba are easy to find but often poorly stocked. If you require any special medication, it is wise to take sufficient supplies with you. Special pharmacies, often open 24 hours a day, are available in major tourist places, but even provincial capitals off the tourist track are poorly provisioned.

 Safe Water Tap water in Cuba is not safe to drink, so make sure you have a constant supply of bottled water, available at hotels, fuel stations and many stores at reasonable prices. Ice in big hotels and resorts is quite safe to consume, but avoid it in cheap restaurants and cafés.

CONCESSIONS

Students/children Unless you are a young person actually studying in Cuba, you will receive no concessions. Cuba is virtually a concession-free zone, but the price of entry to museums and other attractions is generally low.

Senior Citizens There are no concessions.

TRAVELLING WITH A DISABILITY

There are few facilities for visitors with disabilities, though some monuments have access ramps, and many resorts and hotels have wheelchair access to some rooms and amenities. New hotels are being built with disabled access. If you have special requirements, check carefully. Certain destinations, such as the medieval town of Trinidad, are unsuitable for visitors with a disability.

CHILDREN

Cubans generally love children, and if you are travelling with them it will bring you many chance encounters with the locals. All-inclusive resorts have childcare facilities and lots of activities for kids, which makes this type of holiday popular with families.

TOILETS

It is usually possible to use the toilets in hotels and restaurants for a tip – bring tissues or toilet paper.

CUSTOMS

The import of meat or fruit into Cuba is forbidden. The export of more than 23 rolled Cuban cigars must be declared on departure.

EMBASSIES AND HIGH COMMISSIONS

UK ☎ (7) 204-2200

US (Interests Section) ☎ (7) 833-3551

Canada ☎ (7) 204-2516

Germany ☎ (7) 833-2569

Spain ☎ (7) 338025

GREETINGS AND COMMON WORDS

Yes/No **Sí/No**
Please **Por favor**
Thank you **Gracias**
You're welcome **De nada**
Hello **Hola**
Goodbye **Adiós/chao**
Good morning **Buenos días**
Good afternoon **Buenas tardes**
Good night **Buenas noches**
How are you? **¿Qué tal?**
Fine, thank you **Bien, gracias**
How much is this? **¿Cuánto cuesta?**
I'm sorry **Lo siento**
Excuse me **Perdone**
I'd like **Me gustaría**
Open **Abierto**
Closed **Cerrado**
My name is... **Me llamo...**
What's your name? **¿Cómo se llama?**
Pleased to meet you **Mucho gusto**
My pleasure **El gusto es mío**
I'm from... **Soy de...**
Great Britain **Gran Bretaña**
England **Inglaterra**
Scotland **Escocia**
Canada **Canadá**
The United States **Los Estados Unidos**

ACCOMMODATION

Do you have a single/double room?
**¿Le queda alguna habitación individual/
doble?**
with/without bath/toilet/shower
con/sin baño/lavabo/ducha
Does that include breakfast?
¿Incluye desayuno?
Could I see a room?
¿Puedo ver la habitación?
I'll take this room
Me quedo con esta habitación
The key to the room..., please
La llave de la habitación..., por favor
Thank you very much for your hospitality
Muchas gracias por la hospitalidad

DAYS

Today **Hoy**
Tomorrow **Mañana**
Yesterday **Ayer**
Monday **Lunes**
Tuesday **Martes**
Wednesday **Miércoles**
Thursday **Jueves**
Friday **Viernes**
Saturday **Sábado**
Sunday **Domingo**

DIRECTIONS AND TRAVELLING

I'm lost **Me he perdido**
Where is...? **¿Dónde está?**
How do I get to...? **¿Cómo se va...?**
the bank **al banco**
the post office **a la oficina de correos**
the rail station **a la estación de trenes**
Where are the toilets? **¿Dónde están los
servicios?/¿Dónde está el bano?**
Turn left **a la izquierda**
Turn right **a la derecha**
Straight on **todo recto**
At the corner **en la esquina**
At the traffic-lights **en el semáforo**

At the intersection **en la intersección**
Airport **Aeropuerto**
Boat **Barco**
Bus **Guagua/camión**
Bus station **Estación/terminal**
Car **Automóvil/carro**
Church **Iglesia**
Embassy **Embajada**
Hospital **Hospital**
Market **Mercado**
Museum **Museo**
Street **Calle**
Ticket **Boleto**

NUMBERS

0 **cero**	10 **diez**	20 **veinte**	200 **doscientos**
1 **uno**	11 **once**	21 **veintiuno**	300 **trescientos**
2 **dos**	12 **doce**	30 **treinta**	400 **cuatrocientos**
3 **tres**	13 **trece**	40 **cuarenta**	500 **quinientos**
4 **cuatro**	14 **catorce**	50 **cincuenta**	600 **seiscientos**
5 **cinco**	15 **quince**	60 **sesenta**	700 **setecientos**
6 **seis**	16 **dieciséis**	70 **setenta**	800 **ochocientos**
7 **siete**	17 **diecisiete**	80 **ochenta**	900 **novecientos**
8 **ocho**	18 **dieciocho**	90 **noventa**	1,000 **mil**
9 **nueve**	19 **diecinueve**	100 **cien**	

RESTAURANT

I'd like to book a table **¿Me gustaría reservar una mesa?**
A table for... **Una mesa para...**
Have you got a table for two, please? **¿Tienen una mesa para dos personas, por favor?**
Could we see the menu, please? **¿Nos podría traer la carta, por favor?**
Could I have the bill, please? **¿La cuenta, por favor?**

service charge included **servicio incluído**
breakfast **el desayuno**
lunch **el almuerzo**
dinner **la cena**
table **una mesa**
waiter/waitress **camarero/camarera**
starters **los entremeses**
main course **el plato principal**
dessert **postres**
bill **la cuenta**

MENU READER

a elegir of your choice
a la brasa braised
a la parilla grilled
al carbon barbecued
al horno baked
al mojo de ajo in butter and garlic
al vapor steamed
aceituna olive
agua water
aguacate avocado
ajo garlic
arroz rice
asado roasted
atún tuna
azúcar sugar
bacalao cod
bebida drink
bistec steak
bocadillo sandwich
boniato sweet potato
café coffee
caldo soup
camarones shrimp
cangrejo crab
carne meat
cebolla onion
cerdo pork
cerveza beer
champiñones mushroom
chorizo spicy sausage
chuleta chop
cocido stew
cocina kitchen
coco coconut

condimentado (-a) spicy
congrí rice with red beans
cordero lamb
cortado (-a) en cubos diced
crudo rare
dulce sweet
ejotes green (French) beans
empanado (-a) breaded
en escabeche marinated
ensalada salad
entremés hors d'oeuvre
especialidades de la casa house specialities
especialidades locales local specialities
fideos noodles
filete fillet steak
fricasé meat stew
frijoles beans
frito fried
fruta fruit
gaseosas sodas, carbonated drinks
guayaba guava
hamburguesa hamburger
helado ice cream
hervido boiled
hielo ice
huevo egg
huevos fritos/revueltos fried/scrambled eggs

jamón ham
jugo de fruta fruit juice
langosta lobster
leche milk
lechuga lettuce
legumbres vegetables
limón lemon
maíz corn
malanga taro
mantequilla butter
manzana apple
mariscos seafood
mermelada jam
Moros y Cristianos rice with black beans
mortadela sausage
naranja orange
paella seafood and rice casserole
pan bread
papas fritas fries or chips
patatas potato
pepino cucumber
pescado fish
picadillo beef hash
pimienta pepper

piña pineapple
plátano banana
pollo chicken
puerco pork
queso cheese
res beef
ron rum
rosbif roast beef
sal salt
salchicha Vienna sausage
salsa sauce
sopa soup
tasajo salt-dried beef
té tea
ternera veal
tocino bacon
tomate tomato
tortilla omelette
tostada toasted
tostones banana chips
vegetariano vegetarian
vino wine
zanahoria carrot

IF YOU NEED HELP

Help! **¡Socorro! / ¡Ayuda!**
Could you help me, please? **¿Podría ayudarme, por favor?**
Do you speak English? **¿Habla inglés?**
I don't understand **No comprendo**
I don't speak Spanish **No hablo español**
Could you please call a doctor? **¿Podría llamar a un médico, por favor?**

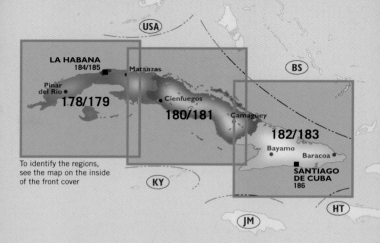

To identify the regions,
see the map on the inside
of the front cover

Regional Maps

▄▄▄	Major route	☐	City
▄▄▄	Motorway	☐	Town/village
▄▄▄	National dual/single	✈	Airport
────	Regional/local road	◧	Featured place of interest
····	Railway	▲	Height in metres
☁	National park		
	Marsh		
····	Restricted area		

178–183

Streetplans

═══	Main road	ⓘ	Tourist information
═══	Other road	◧	Featured place of interest
───	Railway	✝	Church
▬	Important building	✉	Post Office
▬	Park/garden/cemetery	●	Monument/statue
▬	City wall		

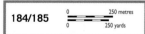

184/185

186

Atlas

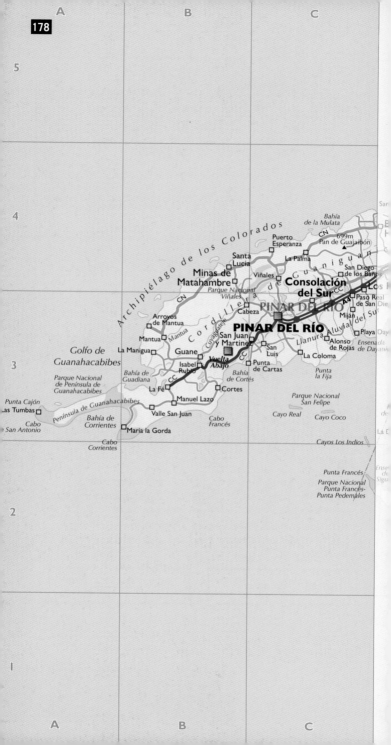

5

4

3

2

I

A   B   C

Archipiélago de los Colorados

Bahía
de la Mulata

CN   699m
Pan de Guajaibón ▲

Puerto
Esperanza

La Palma

Santa
Lucía

San Diego
de los Baños

**Minas de
Matahambre**

Viñales

**Consolación
del Sur**

Parque Nacional
Viñales

Paso Real
de San
Die

CN

Arroyos
de Mantua

Cabeza

PINAR DEL RÍO

Mijan

Playa Day

Mantua

Mantua

PINAR DEL RÍO

Llanura Aluvial del Sur

Ensenada
de Dayan

**Golfo de
Guanahacabibes**

La Manigua

Guane

San Juan
y Martínez

Alonso
de Rojas

San
Luis

Vuelta
Abajo

Isabel
Rubio

La Coloma

Parque Nacional
de Península de
Guanahacabibes

Bahía de
Guadiana

Punta
de Cartas

Punta
la Fija

Cordillera

Guaniguan

Guaniguan

Los

Cn

La D

Cayos Los Indios

Punta Francés

Parque Nacional
Punta Francés-
Punta Pedemales

Punta Cajón

Las Tumbas

Cabo
San Antonio

La Fé

Manuel Lazo

Bahía de
Cortés

Cortes

Parque Nacional
San Felipe

Cayo Real

Cayo Coco

península de Guanahacabibes

Bahía de
Corrientes

Valle San Juan

Cabo
Francés

María la Gorda

Cabo
Corrientes

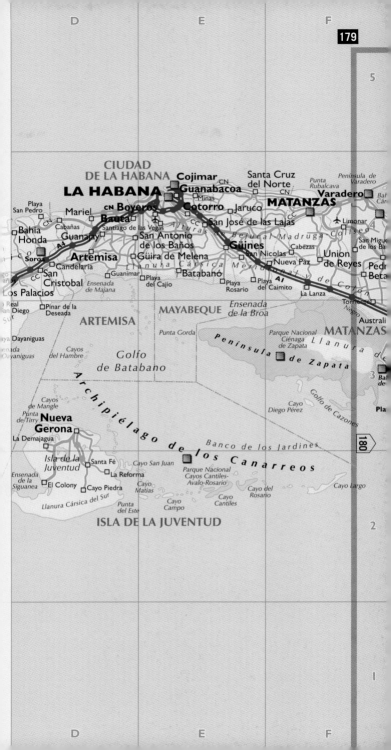

CIUDAD DE LA HABANA

LA HABANA

Cojimar

Guanabacoa

Santa Cruz del Norte

Península de Varadero

Punta Rubalcava

Varadero

Bal Cár

CN Boyeros

Cotorro

Jaruco

MATANZAS

Playa San Pedro

Mariel

Bauta

CN

San José de las Lajas

Minas

Limonar

Coliseo

Bahía Honda

Cabañas

Guanajay

Santiago de las Vegas

San Antonio de los Baños

Güira de Melena

Bejucal

Madruga

San Migu de los Ba

Soroa

CN

CC

Artemisa

Güines

San Nicolas

Cabezas

Union de Reyes

Pedr

Candelaría

Guanímar

Batabanó

Nueva Paz

Beta

San Cristobal

CC

Ensenada de Majana

Playa del Cajio

Playa Rosario

Playa del Caimito

La Lanza

A1

os Palacios

Real San Diego

Piñar de la Deseada

MAYABEQUE

Ensenada de la Broa

Torriente

Negro

Australi

aya Dayaniguas

ARTEMISA

Punta Gorda

MATANZAS

Parque Nacional Ciénaga de Zapata

Llanura

Bal de

nda Dayaniguas

Cayos del Hambre

Golfo de Batabano

Península de Zapata

Pla

Cayos de Mangle

Punta de Tirry

Nueva Gerona

La Demajagua

Cayo Diego Pérez

Golfo de Cazones

Isla de la Juventud

Santa Fé

La Reforma

Cayo San Juan

Banco de los Jardines

Ensenada de la Siguanea

El Colony

Cayo Piedra

Cayo Matias

Parque Nacional Cayos Cantiles-Avalo-Rosario

Cayo del Rosario

Cayo Largo

Llanura Cársica del Sur

Punta del Este

Cayo Campo

Cayo Cantiles

ISLA DE LA JUVENTUD

180

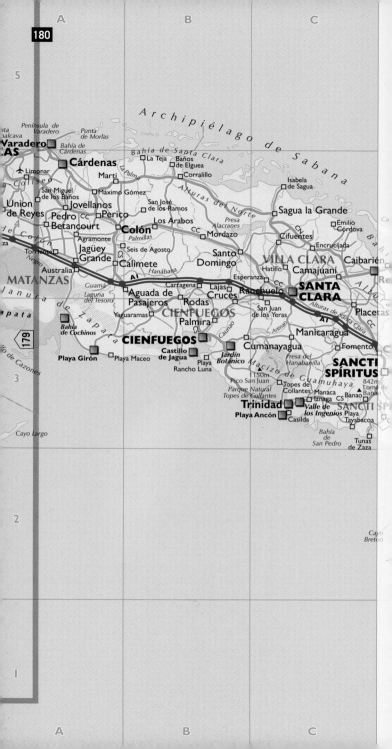

A r c h i p i é l a g o   d e   S a b a n a

Península de Varadero
Punta de Morlas
Punta alcava
Varadero
:AS
Bahía de Cárdenas

Cárdenas
Limonar
Coliseo
Marti
La Teja
Baños de Elguea
Corralillo
Bahía de Santa Clara
La Palma
Isabela de Sagua
Alturas del Norte
San Miguel de los Baños
Máximo Gómez
San José de los Ramos
Sagua la Grande
Union de Reyes
Jovellanos
San Miguel
Presa Alacranes
Emilio Córdova
Pedro CC **Perico**
Los Arabos
Cifuentes
Encrucijada
Betancourt
Agramonte
Colón
CC
Mordazo
CN
MATANZAS
del Colón
Jagüey Grande
Palmillas
Seis de Agosto
Santo Domingo
VILLA CLARA
Caibarién
za
Tormentina
Calimete
Hatillo
Camajuaní
Australia
Hanábana
Esperanza
SANTA CLARA
Re
l a n u r a
Guamá
Cartagena
Lajas
Ranchuelo
CC
Placetas
Laguna del Tesoro
Aguada de Pasajeros
Cruces
Alturas de Santa Clara
Pata
Yaguaramas
Rodas
San Juan de los Yeras
A1
CIENFUEGOS
Palmira
Caunao
Arimao
Manicaragua
Fomento
Bahía de Cochinos
CIENFUEGOS
Cumanayagua
Rio de Cazones
Castillo de Jagua
Jardín Botánico
Presa del Hanabanilla
SANCTI SPÍRITUS
Playa Girón
Playa Maceo
Playa Rancho Luna
Macizo
1150m
842m
Loma de Banao
Pico San Juan
Topes de Collantes
Manaca
Banao
de Guamuhaya
Parque Natural Topes de Collantes
Iznaga
CS
SANCTI
Trinidad
Valle de los Ingenios
SPÍRITUS
Playa Ancón
Casilda
Playa Tayabacoa
Cayo Largo
Bahía de San Pedro
Tunas de Zaza
Cayo Bretón

179

A1

CS

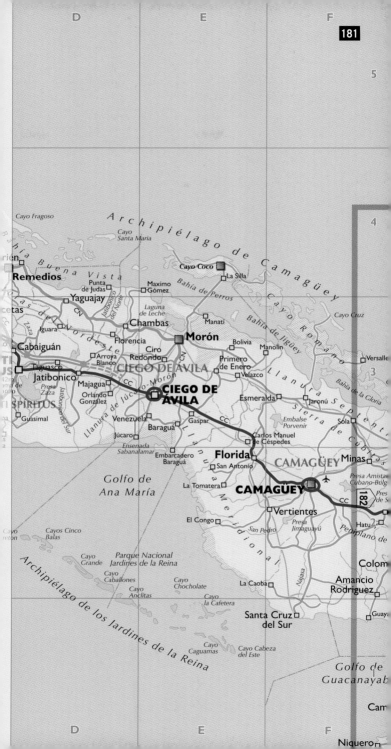

4

Cayo Fragoso

Archipiélago de Camagüey

Cayo Santa María

Cayo Coco

La Silla

Remedios

Vista

Bahía Buena

Punta de Judas

Máximo Gómez

Bahía de Perros

Cayo Romano

Cayo Cruz

Yaguajay

del Norte

Jatibonico

CN

Laguna de Leche

Manatí

Iguara

Chambas

Florencia

Morón

Bolivia

Manolín

Versalle

Cabaiguán

Ciro Redondo

Primero de Enero

Llanura Septentri

Taguasco

Arroya Blanco

CIEGO DE ÁVILA

Velazco

Bahía de la Gloria

Jatibonico

Majagua

CC

CIEGO DE ÁVILA

Esmeralda

Jaronú

Sola

Jibacoa-Morón

Orlando González

Embalse Porvenir

Sierra

Guasimal

Venezuela

Gaspar

CC

Carlos Manuel de Céspedes

Presa Zaza

Jatibonico del Sur

Baraguá

Llanura de Júcaro-Morón

Júcaro

Florida

CAMAGÜEY

Minas

Ensenada Sabanalamar

Embarcadero Baraguá

San Antonio

CAMAGÜEY

Presa Amistad Cubano-Búlg

Golfo de Ana María

La Tomatera

Pres de S

182

Llanura Meridional

Vertientes

Presa Jimaguayú

Hatu

CC

Cayo Breton

Cayos Cinco Balas

El Congo

San Pedro

Peniplano de

Colom

Archipiélago de los Jardines de la Reina

Cayo Grande

Parque Nacional Jardines de la Reina

Cayo Caballones

Cayo Chocholate

La Caoba

Najasa

Amancio Rodríguez

Cayo Anclitas

Cayo la Cafetera

Guay

Santa Cruz del Sur

Cayo Caguamas

Cayo Cabeza del Este

Golfo de Guacanayab

Cam

Niquero

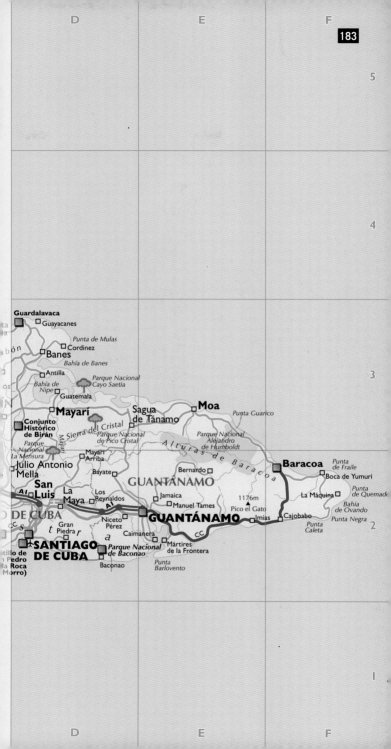

Guardalavaca
Guayacanes
Punta de Mulas
Cordinez
Banes
Bahía de Banes
Antilla
Bahía de
Nipe
Guatemala
Parque Nacional
Cayo Saetia

Mayarí
Sagua
de Tánamo
Moa
Punta Guarico
Conjunto
Histórico
de Birán
Sierra del Cristal
Parque Nacional
de Pico Cristal
Parque Nacional
Alejandro
de Humboldt
Alturas de Baracoa
Parque
Nacional
La Mensura
Mayarí
Arriba
Baracoa
Punta
de Fraile
Boca de Yumurí
Julio Antonio
Mella
Bayate
Bernardo
San
Luis
Los
Reynaldos
Jamaica
1176m
Pico el Gato
La Máquina
Punta
de Quemado
Bahía
de Ovando
Punta Negra
La
Maya
Manuel Tames
DE CUBA
Niceto
Pérez
Imías
Cajobabo
Punta
Caleta
GUANTÁNAMO
Gran
Piedra
**SANTIAGO
DE CUBA**
Caimanera
**Parque Nacional
de Baconao**
Mártires
de la Frontera
Baconao
Punta
Barlovento

astillo de
n Pedro
la Roca
Morro)

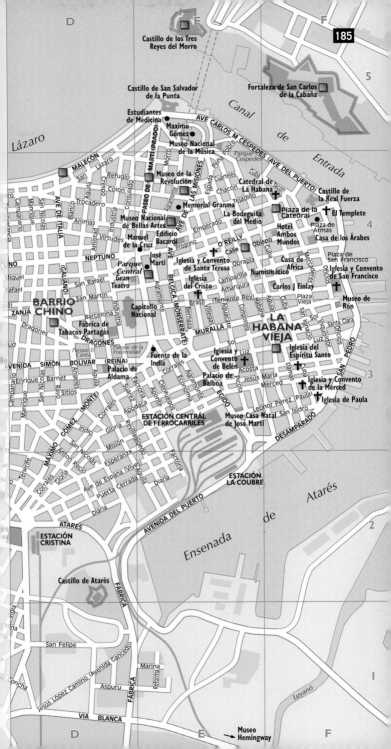

D E F

Castillo de los Tres
Reyes del Morro

5

Fortaleza de San Carlos
de la Cabaña

Castillo de San Salvador
de la Punta

Canal

Estudiantes
de Medicina

Maximo
Gómez

Lázaro

Museo Nacional
de la Música

Parque
Cespedes

de

Entrada

MALECON

Museo de la
Revolución

Catedral de
La Habana

Castillo de
la Real Fuerza

Museo de la
Revolución

Memorial Granma

Plaza de la
Catedral

El Templete

La Bodeguita
del Medio

Museo Nacional
de Bellas Artes

Manuel
de la Cruz

Edificio
Bacardí

Hotel
Ambos
Mundos

Plaza de
Armas

4

Casa de los Árabes

José
Martí

O'REILLY
calle

Obispo

Parque
Central
Gran
Teatro

Iglesia y Convento
de Santa Teresa

Obrapia

Casa de
Africa

Plaza de
San Francisco

BARRIO
CHINO

ZANJA

Iglesia
del Cristo

Lamparilla

Amargura

Numismático

Carlos J Finlay

Iglesia y Convento
de San Francisco

Museo de
Ron

Capitolio
Nacional

Brasil

(Teniente Rey)

Plaza
Vieja

Fábrica de
Tabacos Partagás

MURALLA

LA
HABANA
VIEJA

Fuente de
la India

Iglesia del
Espíritu Santo

AVENIDA SIMÓN BOLIVAR
(REINA)

Palacio
de Aldama

Parque de la
Fraternidad

Iglesia y
Convento de Belén

Acosta

Iglesia y Convento
de la Merced

Palacio de
Balboa

Jesús Maria
Merced

Iglesia de Paula

3

ESTACIÓN CENTRAL
DE FERROCARRILES

Museo Casa Natal
de José Martí

San isidro

DESAMPARADO

ESTACIÓN
LA COUBRE

ATARES

AVENIDA DEL PUERTO

Atarés

2

ESTACIÓN
CRISTINA

Ensenada

de

Castillo de Atarés

FABRICA

San Felipe

Marina

Reforma

Luyanó

1

Jesús López Camino (Avenida Gancedo)

Aspuru

FABRICA

VIA BLANCA

D

E

Museo
Hemingway

F

Santiago de Cuba

LOS OLMOS

Estrella

AVENIDA JUAN GUALBERTO GOMEZ

ANTUNEZ

Frias

Hatuey

Cementerio
Santa Ifigenia

San Magin

Fabrica
de Ron

AVENIDA JUAN GUALBERTO GOMEZ

AVENIDA JESÚS MENÉNDEZ

AVENIDA RENE RAMOS LATOUR

Avenida Mariana Grajales

Martires de Acacia

Avenida de Virginia

General Pérez

Bonifacio Byrne

Andrés

Finlay

Capdevila

El Parque
de los
Muñequitos

Calle 2

Calle 10

Calle 8

Calle 6

Calle 4

Calle 2

AVENIDA PATRICIO LUMUMBA

Rufino

Chávez

Angel Guerra

AVE DE LOS LIBERTADORES

Calle 2

Julian

Miró

del Casals

General

PASEO DE MARTI

PASEO DE MARTI

General
José Maceo

Padre Callejas

10 DE OCTUBRE

M Delgado

Gonzalo

de

Quesada

Narciso López

Mariano Corona

Lacret

Casa del
General G Moncada

Narciso Lopez

Sao del Indio

Moncada

Rodriguez

Los Maceo

AVENIDA DE LOS LIBERTADORES

Casa Natal de
Antonio Maceo

LOS MACEO

Peralejo

J M

Gómez

Sao del Indio

Delgado

FELIX PEÑA

General

Museo
Hernandos
País

General Banderas

Rosado

Pío

General

Monsenor Barnada

Cuarte
Moncad

Saturnino Lora

Iglesia de
Santo Tomás

Teatro
Martí

Hartmann

M

Gómez

PORFIRIO VALIENTE

Mavia

Iglesia de la
Santísima Trinidad

Abel
Santamaria

GENERAL PORTUONDO

L Fuentes

GENERAL PORTUONDO

Máximo Gómez

Máximo Gómez

Edificio
Chivaz

Pal

10 DE OCTUBRE

Iglesia de
San Francisco

Corona

Mariano

General

JUAN BAUTISTA SAGARRA

Sánchez

Hechavarria

AVENIDA DE VICTORIANO

Cultural A
Fernand

Oriente

Cabildo Teatral
Santiago

Monsenor Barnada

AVENIDA DE LOS LIBERTADORES

José a Saco

José a Saco

Ciencas Naturales
T Romay

Juan C zenea

José a Saco

José a Saco

Museo de Ambiente
Histórico Cubano

AGUILERA

Heredia

Balcón de
Velázquez

PADRE PICO

Museo Emilio
Bacardí Moreau

Parque
Céspedes

Galería
Oriente

Palacio
Municipal

Plaza
de Dolores

Museo del
Carnaval

Plaza
de Marte

AGUILERA

ZAMORA

Here

Sala de Conciertos
Dolores

Heredia

Bartolomé Masó

Catedral

Bartolomé Masó

Calle Padre
Pico

Museo de
la Lucha
Clandestina

J Castillo

Duany

Casa Natal
de J M Heredia

Calle
Heredia

AVENIDA 12

DE AGOSTO

Carlos Roloff

GENERAL

General Francisco Pérez

GENERAL JULIO SANGUILY

DIEGO PALACIOS

Museo
del Ron

Iglesia de
Santa Lucía

Castillo

Duany

AVENIDA VALERIANO HIERREZUELO

General Serafín Sánchez

Desiderio Mesnier

PICO

FELIX PEÑA

Mariano Corona

General

Hartmann

Pío

Rosado

PORFIRIO VALIENTE

DIEGO PALACIOS

Mavia

Estrada

Desiderio Mesnier

Hnos Ducasse

Comandante

Borrero

Calixto

García

AVENIDA 24 DE FEBRERO

A Grillo

P E Calano

Villalón

Eduardo
Chibás

Sánchez

General J Rius Rivera

Victor M

AVENIDA 12 DE AGOSTO

P E Bacardí

E de Mesa

Calle 7

Ave General
Pedro Pérez

Carlos M Villalón

CHICHARRONES

Picture credits

The Automobile Association would like to thank the following photographers, companies and picture libraries for their assistance in the preparation of this book.

Abbreviations for the picture credits are as follows: (t) top; (b) bottom; (l) left; (r) right; (AA) AA World Travel Library.

2t Photolibrary; **2tc** AA/D Henley; **2bc** Photolibrary; **2b** Photolibrary; **3t** Photolibrary; **3c** Photolibrary; **3b** © Classic Cuba/ Alamy; **5l** Photolibrary; **5c** © nobleIMAGES/Alamy; **5r** © J Marshall – Tribaleye Images/Alamy; **6/7** Photolibrary; **8** Photolibrary; **9t** © Grant Rooney/Alamy; **9b** © imagebroker/Alamy; **10** © nik wheeler/Alamy; **11** © Chris Cheadle/ Alamy; **12** Mary Evans Picture Library; **14** AA/D Henley; **15** Fidel Castro in the Sierra Maestra Mountains, 1957 (b/w photo),/Private Collection/Peter Newark American Pictures/The Bridgeman Art Library; **16** Photolibrary; **17l** © Alberto Paredes/Alamy; **17r** DESMOND BOYLAN/Reuters/Corbis; **18/9** © Bettmann/CORBIS; **20** NIURKA BARROSO/AFP/Getty Images; **21** AA/D Henley; **22** Photolibrary; **23t** ADALBERTO ROQUE/AFP/Getty Images; **23c** Photolibrary; **23b** © Bill Bachmann/Alamy; **25** Photolibrary; **26** Alexander Hassenstein/Bongarts/Getty Images; **27l** Copyright Sons of Cuba Limited, photograph by Domingo Triana Machín; **27r** STR/AFP/Getty Images; **28l** Photolibrary; **28c** © Michelle Gilders/ Alamy; **28r** © WaterFrame/Alamy; **28/9** © Paul Seheult; Eye Ubiquitous/CORBIS; **30** Popperfoto/Getty Images; **31** Sven Creutzmann/Mambo photo/Getty Images; **32** Peter Stackpole/Time Life Pictures/Getty Images; **33l** AA/D Henley; **33c** © ImageState/Alamy; **33r** AA/D Henley; **45l** Photolibrary; **45c** Photolibrary; **45r** AA/D Henley; **46** Photolibrary; **48** Photolibrary; **49t** Photolibrary; **49b** Photolibrary; **50** Photolibrary; **51** Photolibrary; **52** Photolibrary; **53** Photolibrary; **54** © rgbstudio/Alamy; **56** © Sami Sarkis (2)/Alamy; **57** © Rubens Abboud/Alamy; **58** AA/D Henley; **59** © F1online digitale Bildagentur GmbH/Alamy; **60** © David Cordner/Alamy; **61** © Marla Holden/Alamy; **62b** AA/D Henley; **62t** Photolibrary; **63** age fotostock/Robert Harding; **73l** Photolibrary; **73c** AA/D Henley; **73r** AA/D Henley; **74** Photolibrary; **76** AA/D Henley; **77** Photolibrary; **78/9** Photolibrary; **79** AA/D Henley; **80** AA/C Sawyer; **81** © Robert Harding Picture Library Ltd/ Alamy; **82/3** Photolibrary; **85** Photolibrary; **86** Photolibrary; **87** AA/C Sawyer; **88** © Bill Bachmann/Alamy; **89** Photolibrary; **90** AA/D Henley; **97l** Photolibrary; **97c** AA/C Sawyer; **97r** Mel Longhurst eye ubiquitous/hutchison; **98** Photolibrary; **99** AA/D Henley; **100** Photolibrary; **101** Photolibrary; **102/3** Photolibrary; **104** AA/D Henley; **105** Photolibrary; **106/7** © rgbstudio/Alamy; **108** Photolibrary; **109** Photolibrary; **110/1** Photolibrary; **112/3** Photolibrary; **114/5** © MARKA/ Alamy; **115** Photolibrary; **116** Photolibrary; **117t** Photolibrary; **117b** AA/D Henley; **125l** Photolibrary; **125c** AA/C Sawyer; **125r** AA/C Sawyer; **127t** Ellen Rooney/Robert Harding; **127b** © Larry B Reed/Alamy; **128** AA/D Henley; **129t** Photolibrary; **129b** Photolibrary; **130** Photolibrary; **131** Photolibrary; **132/3** Michael Runkel/Robert Harding; **134** Ellen Rooney/Robert Harding; **135** AA/C Sawyer; **136** Photolibrary; **138/9** Photolibrary; **140** AA/D Henley; **141** AA/D Henley; **142/3** Ellen Rooney/ Robert Harding; **143** Photolibrary; **144** AA/D Henley; **151l** © Classic Cuba/Alamy; **151c** Photolibrary; **151r** AA/D Henley; **152** AA/D Henley; **154** © Melvyn Longhurst/Alamy; **155** John Harden/Robert Harding; **156** © rgbstudio/Alamy; **158** Photolibrary; **160** © Ivan Vdovin/Alamy; **161** © rgbstudio/Alamy; **162** © Ian Nellist/Alamy; **164** © mediacolor's/ Alamy; **165** © Attila Kleb/Alamy; **166** Michael Runkel/Robert Harding; **167** Photolibrary; **169l** © J Marshall - Tribaleye Images/Alamy; **169c** AA/D Henley; **169r** AA/D Henley; **173t** AA/D Henley; **173c** AA/D Henley; **173b** © Kevin Foy/Alamy.

Every effort has been made to trace the copyright holders, and we apologise in advance for any unintentional omissions or errors. We would be pleased to apply any corrections in a following edition of this publication.

SPIRALGUIDE
Questionnaire

Dear Traveller

Your comments, opinions and recommendations are very important to us. Please help us to improve our travel guides by taking a few minutes to complete this simple questionnaire.

You do not need a stamp (unless posted outside the UK). If you do not want to remove this page from your guide, then photocopy it or write your answers on a plain sheet of paper.

Send to: The Editor, Spiral Guides, AA World Travel Guides, FREEPOST SCE 4598, Basingstoke RG21 4GY.

Your recommendations...
We always encourage readers' recommendations for restaurants, night-life or shopping – if your recommendation is used in the next edition of the guide, we will send you a FREE AA Spiral Guide of your choice. Please state below the establishment name, location and your reasons for recommending it.

_____

_____

_____

_____

_____

Please send me AA Spiral _____
(see list of titles inside the back cover)

About this guide...
Which title did you buy?

_____ **AA Spiral**

Where did you buy it? _____

When? m m / y y

Why did you choose an AA Spiral Guide? _____

_____

_____

_____

Did this guide meet your expectations?

Exceeded ☐   Met all ☐   Met most ☐   Fell below ☐

Please give your reasons _____

_____

_____

_____

_____

continued on next page...

Were there any aspects of this guide that you particularly liked?

_____
_____
_____
_____
_____

Is there anything we could have done better?

_____
_____
_____
_____
_____

About you...

Name (Mr/Mrs/Ms) _____

Address _____

_____ **Postcode** _____

Daytime tel no _____ **email** _____

Please _only_ give us your email address and mobile phone number if you wish to hear from us about other products and services from the AA and partners by email or text or mms.

Which age group are you in?

Under 25 ☐   25–34 ☐   35–44 ☐   45–54 ☐   55–64 ☐   65+ ☐

How many trips do you make a year?

Less than one ☐   One ☐   Two ☐   Three or more ☐

Are you an AA member? Yes ☐   No ☐

About your trip...

When did you book? m m / y y   **When did you travel?** m m / y y

How long did you stay? _____

Was it for business or leisure? _____

Did you buy any other travel guides for your trip? ☐ Yes ☐ No

If yes, which ones? _____

_____

Thank you for taking the time to complete this questionnaire. Please send it to us as soon as possible, and remember, you do not need a stamp (unless posted outside the UK).